Anger Management
Games
for Children

Anger Management Games for Children

Deborah M. Plummer

Illustrations by Jane Serrurier

Jessica Kingsley Publishers
London and Philadelphia

First published in 2008
by Jessica Kingsley Publishers
116 Pentonville Road
London N1 9JB, UK
and
400 Market Street, Suite 400
Philadelphia, PA 19106, USA
www.jkp.com

Library of Congress Cataloging in Publication Data
A CIP catalog record for this book is available from the Library of Congress

British Library Cataloguing in Publication Data
A CIP catalogue record for this book is available from the British Library

ISBN 978 1 84310 628 9

Printed and bound in Great Britain by
Athenaeum Press, Gateshead, Tyne and Wear

Contents

Part One: Theoretical and practical background

Part Two: Games for anger management

List of games

Part One

Theoretical and practical background

1

Introduction

What is anger management?

Imagine the following scene: Brenda is preparing to walk with her three-year-old son, Ryan and her daughter Hayley (seven) to Hayley's school. They normally go by car but today they have to get the bus. They are running late because Hayley can't find her shoes. Brenda dresses Ryan while calling instructions to Hayley. They set off to the bus stop. Hayley is chatting to her mum about school but Brenda is pre-occupied with Ryan who doesn't want to hold her hand and keeps pulling away from her. They walk past the park and Ryan sees the swings. He suddenly screeches 'No! No more walk!' and sits down on the pavement kicking his legs furiously. He manages to kick his mum as she tries to pick him up. Brenda shouts at Ryan. Hayley starts to cry and throws down her book bag with such force that her reading book falls out and lands in a puddle.

It is conceivable that Hayley might have a pretty miserable start to her school day! Ryan may quickly forget his frustration if he is distracted and reassured, but his sister is old enough to brood on the various events of the morning. Her thoughts may fuel anxiety (Will I get into trouble because of the reading book? Will I be late for school?) and feelings of anger (It's Ryan's fault, he gets all the attention). These mixed emotions may in turn affect her concentration and performance in the classroom and may even lead to an uncharacteristic display of anger toward another child. In this instance 'Super Mum' Brenda retrieves the situation with a bit of expert mothering! She hugs Ryan, acknowledges his frustration and distracts his attention from the swings. She simultaneously cuddles Hayley, apologizes for not paying attention to her (she is, after all, 'Super Mum'!), rescues the book, acknowledges Hayley's feelings of anxiety, reassures her, and still manages to get everyone to the bus stop on time!

The anger and frustration felt by Hayley, Ryan and Brenda are all normal responses to an accumulation of events. Anger management strategies were put into place quickly and Ryan and Hayley learned the value of self-calming through their mother's support and model. Of course, anger management is not always as easy as

Brenda might have us think! However, such common scenarios illustrate three important points for consideration:

- Anger is a normal, healthy human emotion.

- Young children need help in learning how to manage feelings of anger successfully.

- Anger in children is not something to be feared, denied or repressed.

These points are explored in more depth in Chapter 2: Understanding anger. I believe that they should inform our interactions with all children – those who are coping with normal levels of anger as well as those who are experiencing anger frequently, inappropriately or too intensely or whose anger lasts for long periods of time.

In order to help children to understand and manage angry feelings successfully we must also be aware of our own strengths and needs in relation to this emotion and be prepared to examine our personal beliefs about how to manage it appropriately. With these aims in mind, *Anger Management Games for Children* sets out to explore some of the information now available to us about anger, its origins and its consequences. It offers ways for adults to develop or increase their ability to feel comfortable with children's anger and to reflect on their interactions with children, and it shows how youngsters can learn the skills for anger management through a natural childhood activity: playing games.

Who will benefit from anger management games?

The games are suitable for all children from 5–12 years of age. In the school setting they will fit into a wide selection of personal, social and health education (PSHE) and other learning objectives. They can be used to teach and enhance a variety of skills at primary level and to reinforce strategies for anger management during the vulnerable period of transition to secondary education. The material can be incorporated into individual behaviour plans (IBPs) and can be used to target specific aspects of individual education plans (IEPs).

Children attending after school clubs, youth groups and play schemes will also enjoy and benefit from engaging in the activities and crucially, all the games can be played at home by families.

The material will also complement intervention methods used in a diverse range of therapy approaches with individual children or groups, including existing anger management strategies. *However, the games alone should not be viewed as a substitute for professionally led anger management programmes when children have been assessed as having severe or complex emotional needs.*

Why use non-competitive games?

I have chosen to focus on non-competitive games where the enjoyment and the challenge come from the process itself rather than from winning. This is not because I have an aversion to competitive games. In fact, far from this being the case, I do believe that there is a place for these once a child is ready to engage in them and does so by her own choice. The child's world is after all a competitive arena and most children will naturally play games of skill that involve winning or losing or being 'in' or 'out' whether we adults encourage them or not. Younger children and those who are particularly vulnerable to low self-esteem will often find these win or lose games extremely difficult to cope with, however. For such children, the anticipation of the 'rewards' of winning might be so great that the disappointment of losing has an equally dramatic effect on their mood. In order to enjoy and benefit from competitive games they will therefore need to first develop a certain degree of emotional resilience, competence and self-efficacy, all of which can be fostered initially through non-competitive activities.

How to use this book

The games and activities are divided into nine sections, including warm-ups and wind-downs. In some instances the division is slightly arbitrary since many of the games could be placed in more than one section and you will find that you are often touching on several aspects of anger management within just one game. However, if you keep the principal focus in mind this will help you to evaluate and adapt individual games appropriately.

Each game has been marked with a set of symbols to aid in the selection of the most appropriate ones for different groups of children:

⑤	This gives an indication of the suggested *youngest* age for playing the game. There is no upper age limit.
⏱ 10 mins	An approximate time is given for the length of the game (excluding the discussion time). This will obviously vary according to the size of group and the ability of the players.
♦ ♦ ♦	Indicates that the game is suitable for larger groups (eight or more).
♦ ♦	The game is suitable for small groups.
♡♡♡	The game involves a lot of speaking unless it is adapted.
♡♡	A moderate amount of speaking is required by players.
♡	The game is primarily a non-verbal game or one requiring minimal speech.
☑ listening	This gives an indication of a skill used or developed by playing this game.

The lists of skills for each game have been limited to just a few key areas, but you may find that you want to add others relevant to your own focus of work. Undoubtedly, the more often that you play these games, the more skills you will want to add to each list!

Adaptations

Ideas for expanding and adapting the games are offered as a starting point for your own experimentation with the main themes. Most games can be adapted appropriately to enable children with diverse strengths and needs to take part. Older children should also be given plenty of opportunities to adapt games by inventing new versions or altering the rules in discussion with other group members. This helps them to understand the value of rules and to distinguish more easily between what works and what doesn't. Discussion with peers also provides valuable experience of negotiating and developing flexibility in decision making. It is of course important to make it clear beforehand that there are certain safety and non-discriminatory rules governing the invention or changing of games which must be followed.

Reflections and notes

Suggestions for reflection and for discussion with older children are provided after each game description. Sometimes even the briefest time spent in reflecting on behaviour and feelings or on actions and consequences can help children to make enormous leaps in realization. Equally, children who play games regularly will often start to gain insights into their own behaviour and emotions and those of others purely through the experience, and will not necessarily need to take specific time to reflect on what happened within every session.

As a general principle I would suggest that we should not give more time to a discussion at the time of playing than we do to the game itself. However, these topics do also provide an opportunity for drawing links between different themes at later times. You could remind children of particular games when this is relevant: 'Do you remember when we played that game of… What did you feel when…?'

The suggestions for discussion can also provide focus points for you to use during your own planning and reflection sessions (see pages 47–49 for further guidelines). To aid this process, each game description includes space for you to add your own notes. These might include such things as personal insights and experiences of using the games, personal preferences, dislikes, problems and successes.

Additional notes

Finally, because you will undoubtedly have many more games in your repertoire and will gather extra ideas from colleagues and children, each section ends with a blank summary page for 'additional notes'. Here you can add to your list and make any further general comments on your experiences with the games you have used.

My hope is that this format will encourage reflective practice but that it will not *dis*courage enjoying the pure fun of playing games with young children. This, after all, is the essential value of games – having fun while learning about ourselves and others!

Integrating games into different settings

The ways in which the games are adapted and incorporated into family life and into educational and therapy approaches can and should vary according to the setting and according to the needs, strengths and experiences of the children. Each adult who facilitates games will naturally bring his or her own personality, imagination, expertise and knowledge to the games and create something new from the basic format. In this way, playing with the process of playing becomes an integral part of our own learning.

However, the games in this book do follow a logical progression. If you are structuring games sessions based specifically around anger management, I therefore suggest that each session starts with a warm-up game, followed by two or three games from one of the outlined sections (or from two consecutive sections), and finishing with a relaxation/wind-down game.

Warm-ups and ice-breakers foster group cohesion and help to develop a group identity. They encourage children to interact with each other, and help them to feel that they have been acknowledged by everyone else. They act as a ritual to mark the beginning of a session and to ensure that each person has fully 'arrived' in the group.

The relaxations and wind-downs emphasize the skills involved in managing levels of emotion and teach simple strategies for 'letting go' of any left over feelings which may have manifested during earlier games and discussions, or which may arise in the future. This combination is important because children need to feel safe and contained when they are exploring emotions. The structure of a games session can facilitate this by providing predictability and certainty.

Further guidelines for facilitating the games can be found in Chapter 4: Structuring the emotional environment.

Facing up to anger

The conscious control of anger is a complex process and we cannot expect children to manage this without support and guidance. Aristotle summed up this conundrum very succinctly:

> Anyone can become angry – that is easy. But to be angry with the right person, to the right degree, at the right time, for the right purpose, and in the right way – this is not easy. (Aristotle, The Nicomachean Ethics (cited in Goleman 1996))

The task for adults is to recognize the need for all children to develop a healthy approach to anger management and to take up the challenge!

2

Understanding anger

Key points

- Anger is a normal, healthy human emotion.

- Young children need help in learning how to manage feelings of anger successfully.

- The foundations for emotional regulation are laid down in infancy.

- The way in which a child interprets situations and events has important implications for anger management.

- Anger in children is not something to be feared, denied or repressed.

- Most anger occurs in the context of a trigger event or is secondary to another underlying emotion.

- There are several core elements which are crucial to the development of healthy anger management in childhood.

Anger is a normal, healthy human emotion.

For many of us, 'childhood anger' conjures up images of aggression and of children who are 'out of control' or 'disaffected' or 'troubled'. We are bombarded with images and stories of such aggression on an almost daily basis, and teachers will be all too aware of the thousands of children who face school exclusion every year because of disruptive behaviour.

It is unfortunate that in this climate, fear of the consequences of unrestrained anger has led many adults to become anxious about coping with *any* displays of anger, even that of very young children. This much misunderstood emotion has seemingly become the 'bad apple' of the emotions' family, something to be controlled, eradicated or suppressed.

But of course, what we are talking about here is the inappropriate *manifestation* of angry feelings. Anger in itself is not necessarily an unwelcome emotion. In fact, it can sometimes be a force for positive change. When it is expressed appropriately and meaningfully it can be a perfectly normal and healthy response to injustice, for example, and can act as an energizer and a motivator for action. Anger is also a basic survival response that enables us to react instantly to threatening situations and to defend ourselves in times of crises.

We must also remember that the word 'anger' covers a whole range of emotional intensity including mild irritation or frustration. It is therefore something that we are likely to come across in others or to experience in ourselves on a fairly regular basis. If we handle it successfully then we can help children to understand that anger need not be a frightening, unpredictable or overwhelming experience and that they do have the capacity to control this emotion in a productive and healthy manner.

Young children need help in learning how to manage feelings of anger successfully.

It is clear that anger management strategies must do much more than simply offer ways of controlling or suppressing angry outbursts. The challenge for adults is to help children to develop the key skills and capacities for emotional regulation – a task which starts in babyhood and continues throughout the early years. As children learn to negotiate the world we can help them to develop skills of empathy and cooperation, support their growing ability to tolerate frustration, and help them to develop appropriate strategies for self-calming when they are anxious. With these foundations in place children will then be more able to channel justified anger into appropriate responses and to recognize and defuse inappropriate manifestations of this powerful emotion.

The foundations for emotional regulation are laid down in infancy.

One of the primary developmental tasks in the emotional life of a young child is the establishment of an effective emotion-regulation system: the ability to self-regulate and self-calm so that he or she is not constantly overwhelmed with difficult emotions.

During babyhood, it is sensitive and aware parenting which supports this process. We now know that both positive and negative interactions between babies and their caregivers can directly affect the delicate chemical balance and neurological structure of the infant's rapidly developing brain. Parents who are attuned to their baby's feelings will automatically provide the comfort and touch which allows the emotion-regulation system to develop and to function effectively. But research shows that where this natural process is inhibited there may be long-term consequences:

> Stress in infancy – such as consistently being ignored when you cry – is particularly hazardous because high levels of cortisol in the early months of life can also affect the development of other neurotransmitter systems whose pathways are still being established… When stressed, these various biochemical systems may become skewed in ways that make it more difficult for the individual to regulate himself in later life. (Gerhardt 2004, p.65)

Levels of hormones such as oxytocin (the hormone known to aid the 'bonding' process after childbirth) and serotonin (the 'feel-good' hormone that helps us to relax) also vary enormously according to how much positive physical contact children experience. The release of oxytocin triggered by positive touch contributes to feelings of safety and comfort and is associated with the regulation of cortisol. High levels of cortisol on the other hand can cause us to feel:

> overwhelmed, fearful, and miserable, colouring our thoughts, feelings, and perceptions with a sense of threat or dread as if everything we need to do is far too hard. (Sunderland 2006, p.87)

Our early experiences also profoundly affect the development of the pre-frontal cortex – the area of the brain that deals with feelings and with social interactions. The pre-frontal cortex plays a vital role in inhibiting or regulating the more primitive responses of the amygdala – the area of the brain which deals with the fear and self-defence systems.

Without a well-developed pre-frontal cortex we will have difficulty with self-control and self-regulation and also with the ability to feel 'connected' to others. This is why very young children are unable to control their impulses to 'lash out' or have a temper tantrum – because the pre-frontal cortex is not yet fully developed.

This area of the brain is most vulnerable to outside influences during its critical period of development in the first four years of life. Such influences include the parents' ability to tune into their child's feelings. Studies have shown that four-year-olds who have been brought up in chaotic and stressful environments (for example where there has been neglect or abuse) have a measurably smaller pre-frontal cortex compared to four-year-olds who have experienced a nurturing environment. These children show clear signs of lack of social competence, an inability to manage stress and the inability to see things from another child's viewpoint (Gerhardt 2004).

Although negative experiences may make it extremely difficult for a child to regulate her emotions when she is older, there is fortunately much that can be done to redress the damage. The brain is remarkable in its capacity to adapt and respond to new influences, particularly during early childhood. Supportive interactions and the teaching of key skills can therefore greatly enhance a previously stressed child's capacity for self-control, self-regulation and connection to others.

The way in which a child interprets situations and events has important implications for anger management.

With increasing maturity, a child's thought processes and the ways in which she appraises situations will start to play a bigger part in how she interprets and regulates her emotions. When she experiences a state of arousal, such as in anger, she will look at her immediate environment for an explanation and will also draw on past events and 'emotion memories'. Although the links that she makes may be largely subconscious, they can still inform her present reactions. In this way, unpleasant or out of control experiences of feeling angry in the past may, for instance, intensify her current physiological arousal, which in turn confirms her appraisal of the situation and intensifies her experience of the emotion.

Different *types* of anger are also known to produce essentially different activation responses in the brain. For example, when we are under attack and need to defend ourselves, the body reduces the production of serotonin and produces high levels of norepinephrine. This hormone, also known as noradrenaline, plays an important part in preparing the body for action in an emergency. In irritable aggression on the other hand both serotonin *and* norepinephrine are reduced (Gerhardt 2004).

The flood of stress hormones through the body during a strong anger response can often leave a child with a chemical 'after effect' which may cause physical shaking or feelings of nausea, even after the anger has subsided. This 'emotional menu' of physiological responses has implications for how we structure our support at different stages of a child's anger and in accordance with different types and degrees of anger manifestation.

The influence of past experiences and the developing capacity to appraise situations as potentially threatening or stressful, combined with fluctuations in biochemical levels and the complex interactions between the pre-frontal cortex and the amygdala all conspire to make emotional regulation a real challenge for all of us. It is hardly surprising that children find this a tricky developmental task. Nor is it surprising that some children have persistent 'problems' in managing anger. The need for adults to support *all* children in developing appropriate emotional self-regulation skills from babyhood onwards is clear.

Anger in children is not something to be feared, denied or repressed.
As we have seen, the ways in which children experience feelings of anger and the ways in which they express these feelings are partly determined by their developmental level and partly reinforced by the reactions of others and by family patterns and past experiences. Most children are able to let go of anger fairly quickly, but some may begin to believe that this is the only way that they will get what they want because that is what their experience has taught them.

Persistent anger can lead to feelings of confusion and can be a frightening and lonely experience. Inappropriate expressions of anger by children are likely to engender negative responses from adults and peers alike. Classmates will tend to avoid persistently angry children and this can lead to social isolation and strong feelings of inadequacy. In extreme situations, a child's problems with managing anger can lead to truancy, school exclusion and self-hatred.

Children who experience out of control anger often look to adults to give them a sense of containment and safety. If this need is not met, they may become more and more anxious and their angry behaviour will increase in their desperate attempt to gain attention and recognition of their distress.

Informal observations of children at play will quickly reveal that whereas some youngsters are more prone to direct expression of anger either verbally or physically, others are more likely to repress their anger or to express it indirectly (e.g. through tears). Sometimes this repression is a learned response due to the disapproval of caregivers or to experiences of being rejected when anger is shown. Constant repression or denial of anger can be detrimental to a child's emotional and physical well-being. It may for example lead to depression in later life and has also been linked with lowered immunity due to chronically high levels of stress hormones, particularly cortisol, in the body (Gerhardt 2004).

Children who suppress their anger may never learn the skills for emotional regulation. They may become unaware of what they are feeling, not just when they are angry but in relation to pleasurable emotions as well.

These two extremes in handling feelings of anger are destructive to the individual in different ways. Teaching children healthy anger management skills is an absolute necessity in order to counteract these tendencies.

Most anger occurs in the context of a trigger event or is secondary to another underlying emotion.

While there are some children who do seem to be constantly angry, most instances of childhood anger can be traced to a 'trigger' event or an underlying emotion such as frustration, sadness or anxiety. In helping children to manage angry feelings we therefore need to be aware of the contexts in which these feelings might be generated. The main areas for consideration are outlined below.

Threats to self-esteem

This is perhaps one of the most important connections to consider when looking at anger management issues. The link between self-esteem and aggressive behaviour and depression has long been recognized. Children who have specific behavioural difficulties for example, often seek out opportunities to confirm their feelings of low self-worth by entering into conflict with others or by behaving in a way that invites rejection (Booker 1999).

Healthy levels of self-esteem correlate with the sort of positive outlook that allows a child to cope with many of life's difficulties without feeling 'got at' or victimized. However, when self-esteem is low, the threshold for anger may also be low and an angry response can easily be triggered by a minor infraction or an unintentional slight. Supporting healthy self-esteem is of primary importance in any anger management strategy.

Stress

There are many aspects of daily life which young children find physically, emotionally or mentally stressful for short periods of time. Small amounts of positive stress are normal and help a child to feel motivated to achieve. But where stress is excessive or continuous over a long period of time, even at relatively low levels, then he will experience a 'toxic' build up of stress hormones such as cortisol, and angry feelings will be engendered much more easily.

Margot Sunderland highlights the importance of helping children to manage intense feelings in order to minimize the negative effects of stress when they are older:

> When a child is not helped enough with his intense feelings, the alarm systems in his lower brain can be over-active in later life. This means that he may over-react

to minor stressors, 'sweat the small stuff', and live a life of worrying, and/or be angry or short-tempered for much of the time. (Sunderland 2006, p.27)

Continuous stress of this sort may be due to such things as ongoing bullying, anxiety about a parent who has a chronic illness, uncertainty or unpredictability at home or pressure to achieve beyond his capabilities. Persistent understimulation (boredom) can also register in the brain as stress. Whereas adults are able to do something to relieve boredom, young children have fewer choices about how to do this and may resort to temper tantrums or fighting with siblings.

Another, often misunderstood, area of stress is related to communication disorders. While a lot of children seem to cope with speech or language impairment with remarkable fortitude, there are some who become acutely troubled by feelings of anger rooted in the inherent frustrations of their communication difficulty. For example, many such children have difficulty in negotiating with others and in verbally 'standing up' for themselves when they have been unfairly accused or their talents and successes go unrecognized. Children with severe language impairments often do not have the vocabulary to label or describe complex emotions or the internal language capacity (self-talk) to help themselves to regulate their emotions.

These children, often stressed to breaking point on a daily basis, may feel that they have very little control over their lives and very little control over the turmoil of emotions that threatens to erupt at unpredictable moments. Their frustration may lead to anger directed against themselves or against those who don't understand them, at the 'systems' that don't allow them to communicate effectively, or at those who don't take the time to stop and listen.

Insecurity

The link between parent and child attachment patterns and the child's later ability to self-regulate has been the focus for much research. For example, an early relationship that is harsh or punitive may result in an insecure avoidant attachment where the child avoids contact with their caregiver, rather than seeking contact, when they are anxious. Children experiencing this type of relationship are much more likely to be aggressive when they are older (e.g. Renkin et al. 1989 cited in Gerhardt 2004 p.174).

Similarly, uncertainty in the constancy of the primary caregiver can continue to manifest itself later in childhood as anger directed against other adults, including teachers. These children often want support and attention but at the same time become anxious in the presence of adults, an ambiguous state that can result in anger when a caring adult tries to help.

Sadness

Profound sadness, for example due to the loss of a family member, can make a child more vulnerable to bouts of unexplained anger as they battle with feelings of abandonment and uncertainty. Extensive research with adolescents suffering from periods of depression shows a strong correlation between feelings of deep sadness and feelings of anger (Harter 1999). This research also offers insights into how younger children often experience a blend of these two emotions.

Frustration

I have already mentioned frustration in connection with communication difficulties, but of course frustration is an inevitable part of the developmental hurdles that all children must negotiate. Youngsters will have countless experiences of feeling frustrated when they cannot have something or cannot do something because they are too little, too young or don't yet have the necessary knowledge or dexterity. Older children may experience frustration when something they have spent a long time over is spoiled accidentally or their hard work is not acknowledged. Children who have a tendency towards 'perfectionism' can easily become frustrated and destroy their own work when they make a small mistake.

While most children learn to tolerate a certain amount of frustration as they get older, when such feelings are frequent or the child has not developed a healthy degree of emotional resilience, then either self-directed anger or anger towards others is a likely consequence. These children often find it hard to ask for help with a task before frustration sets in – asking for assistance may be closely linked with fear of (or confirmation of) failure, thus compounding feelings of inadequacy and low self-worth. Simply telling a child that it is 'OK to ask' may not be sufficient to help them to get over this hurdle.

Psychotherapist Sue Gerhardt summarizes the research in this area, pointing out that the three main skills involved in controlling impulses appear to be the ability to self-distract, the ability to seek information about the obstacles to the desired goals and the use of comfort-seeking strategies:

> One study found that 3-year-olds who were skilled in using all three strategies showed the least aggressive and externalizing behaviour (Gilliom *et al.* 2002). They were able to control themselves sufficiently to turn away from the source of frustration and focus on something else, and were less likely to attack it. They could also ask questions about when the situation would be alleviated, which was very helpful in dissolving anger. (Gerhardt 2004, p.179)

In this study, children who were not able to use all three strategies were found to be the most aggressive.

The contributing factors described above are often masked or overshadowed by the actual displays of anger in young children – the original source of a child's angry feelings may go unrecognized, with more emphasis being made of the perception that she has 'trouble with anger'. The child herself may not even recognize the original trigger and may be unable to explain why she hit out or lost her temper with a friend.

We therefore need to be aware that such factors may be contributing to a child's distress, particularly where she is persistently or uncharacteristically angry.

Other, more immediate triggers to anger include:

- jealousy and sibling rivalry
- a sense of being treated unfairly, e.g. punished for something that they didn't do
- embarrassment
- disappointment
- an adult intervening to 'help out' when this was not needed
- seeing injustice done to others
- humiliation
- loss of control/ sense of autonomy
- lack of understanding by others (empathy)
- lack of child's ability to empathize with others
- others denying or rejecting the child's genuine feelings
- hunger (low blood sugar levels)
- tiredness
- illness/pain.

There are several core elements which are crucial to the development of healthy anger management in childhood.

In exploring the various theories of the nature of anger it becomes clear that there are certain foundation elements which help a child to successfully manage angry feelings. These are:

- Self-awareness – a child's ability to be aware of the emotional feeling as it arises and aware of the thought that goes with it.
- The language ability to be able to name the emotion that she is experiencing.

- The ability to successfully communicate (e.g. verbally or with assisted communication techniques) what it is that she wants.

- Self-control – her belief that she has some control over her feelings and over the ways in which she expresses them.

- Empathy – her ability to see things from another person's point of view.

- Effective listening skills – her ability to really hear what others are saying and to reflect on this.

- The ability to reflect on her own behaviour and on the consequences of that behaviour.

- Problem-solving, cooperation and negotiation skills.

- The ability to self-distract and self-calm.

Although in general these develop with maturation, their growth is also dependent on and supported by sensitive parenting and teaching. All these elements are addressed by the games described in Part Two.

3

Why use games to support healthy anger management?

Key points

- Play is a serious business!
- Games provide structure and predictability and can offer a safe environment for the exploration of emotions.
- Games reflect aspects of real life. The ways in which children engage in them often reflects their approach to life in general.
- Games provide valuable learning opportunities in many different areas of social and personal development.

Play is a serious business!

Why is it that some games seem to 'work' well with one group and not with another? I believe that one of the main reasons lies in how well the person who is facilitating the games understands the importance of the game process and how powerful this process can be. Of course, games played as energizers or treats can be exciting and fun and a source of immense pleasure for the players. Occasionally, however, they can also be sheer torture for the quiet child, the child who has difficulty understanding the rules of games, the child who is already full of pent up frustration or anxiety, or who fears being 'left out' or losing yet again. In contrast, a well-chosen game played with awareness on the part of the facilitator can be an incredibly effective instrument for supporting a child's emergent sense of self and for helping him to tolerate frustration and learn to cooperate with his peers.

Games provide a fun way of learning serious ideas and important life skills. When they are facilitated by adults, for example in a therapeutic or teaching environment, they should always be played mindfully and with integrity. We need to be fully aware of why we are playing the games that we have chosen; fully conscious of the possible effects that playing such games might have; and fully 'present' with the children in order to understand their ways of responding and interacting and to appreciate the spontaneous learning that is occurring within and between group members.

The universality of play and traditional games highlights the developmental importance of this aspect of children's learning, and the building of emotional, physical and cognitive skills. From early babyhood, through our childhood years and often into adulthood (through sports activities for example) play is how we find out about ourselves and the world. This process begins through manipulation of our own body (e.g. sucking a thumb or toes); play with sounds (babbling); play with objects (e.g. a comfort blanket or a soft toy) and play with significant people in our lives (e.g. the 'mirroring' of facial expression and body movements that often occurs so naturally between a parent and child, games of peek-a-boo and waving 'bye bye'). In this way we gradually learn what is 'me' and 'not me', we learn the rudiments of cause and effect and turn-taking. We even learn to cope with feelings of temporary separation and loss with games such as hide-and-seek and peek-a-boo.

From this type of play we move on gradually to symbolic play – manipulation of objects as symbols of real things – and then to imaginary play where some props may be used but much, or all, of the scenario is imagined. This type of engagement in the world of imagination gradually moves from solitary or parallel play to engagement in play with others: 'I'm the Mummy and I have to feed the baby', 'I will be the princess and you can be the wicked witch' or 'I'm a policeman and I'm looking for a robber'.

By working our imagination like a muscle we learn to problem-solve, to tolerate frustration, to work through some of life's difficulties and so reach our own 'child-level' of understanding of the complexities of the world – we make 'child-sense' of our experiences in a simplified and safe way and thereby strengthen our emotional resilience.

Play of one sort or another provides invaluable opportunities for children to learn through imitation, to experience the consequences of their actions and to experiment with different skills and different outcomes without fear of failure or being judged unfavourably by others. Play is also a medium through which children can expand and consolidate their language skills.

Psychologist Catherine Garvey suggests that:

> because playing is voluntarily controlled (executed in a way in which imperfect achievement is minimally dangerous), its effects are probably intricately related to the child's mastery and integration of his experiences…when the behaviour is next performed in a non-play mode, it may be more skilled, better integrated, and associated with a richer or wider range of meaning. In this way play can contribute to the expertise of the player and to his effectiveness in the non-play world. (Garvey 1977, p.118)

Vivian Paley has also documented many crucial observations of the importance of children's play. As a nursery teacher she became increasingly aware of how children in her classes placed a great deal of emphasis on things that happened during play activities – it was the themes that arose during play that they were most likely to want to discuss. In her wonderful book *The Boy Who Would Be a Helicopter* Paley observes that children's rites and images in play:

> seem mainly concerned with the uses of friendship and fantasy to avoid fear and loneliness and to establish a comfortable relationship with people and events. In play, the child says, 'I can *do* this well; I can *be* this effectively; I *understand* what is happening to me and to other children'. (Paley 1991, p.10)

Play during childhood can stimulate a 'playful' approach to life at a later age, including the ability to bring humour and fun to relationships and to see life's difficulties as challenges rather than insurmountable obstacles. It helps children to develop social awareness and conscience and creates opportunities to explore concepts of fairness and equality.

As with all areas of emotional and social development, we now know that pleasurable, playful experiences affect the chemical balance and neurological make-up of the brain. For example, imaginative and creative play is known to lower levels of stress chemicals, enabling children to deal more successfully with stressful situations. Gentle rough and tumble play and laughter are also known to have anti-stress effects, activating the brain's emotion-regulating centres and causing the release of opioids, the natural brain chemicals that induce feelings of pleasure and well-being (Sunderland 2006).

Games provide structure and predictability and can offer a safe environment for the exploration of emotions.

How do games fit into this magical world of play? Garvey defines games as play activities that are structured with 'explicit rules that can be precisely communicated' (1977, p.101). The ability to play games with rules usually emerges at around five or six years of age although, as outlined above, the early signs of this can be seen with very young infants (a game of peek-a-boo for example involves structured turn-taking to some extent and children of three often understand the 'unspoken' rules of familiar games). By around five years of age children are more able to tolerate waiting and a degree of inevitable frustration at being 'out' in a competitive game. They are beginning to exercise self-control and the ability to follow rules and conventions. They are also more able to sustain interactions with others for longer periods.

Games generally have clear start and finishing points and follow sequences which are accepted by the players and which can therefore be replicated at other times and in different situations. These 'process' rules provide a sense of predictability and security even when the game itself might be a bit scary, and in this way various real life issues which might be too difficult or painful to confront head on can be played out in safety. Such games may perhaps even engender laughter and enjoyment whilst nevertheless tackling important life issues.

Opie and Opie conducted extensive research into children's street games in the 1960s. They observed that:

> Children like games in which there is a sizeable element of luck, so that individual abilities cannot be directly compared. They like games which restart almost automatically, so that everybody is given a new chance. They like games which move in stages, in which each stage, the choosing of leaders, the picking-up of sides, the determining of which child shall start, is almost a game in itself…many of the games, particularly those of young children, are more akin to ceremonies than competitions. In these games children gain the reassurance that comes with repetition, and the feeling of fellowship that comes from doing the same as everyone else. (Opie and Opie 1976, pp.394–95)

Games allow children to explore the function of rules and conventions and to safely test the boundaries of what is acceptable to others within a rule-governed activity. In their daily lives children constantly have to negotiate their way through a welter of adult-imposed rules, structures and boundaries. Sometimes these are explicit, but often they are unclear or unspoken, taken for granted by the adults but a potential minefield for children who forget, don't know or don't understand them. Constant insistence on adherence to adult imposed rules in games may similarly have a negative effect on the process, resulting in children disengaging with the games, rebelling or becoming passive. Rules should therefore be flexible enough to accommodate different types or levels of response.

A major way in which children will learn to understand and respect rules is by having experience of devising them for themselves, preferably by negotiating with others, and then trying them out. In this way they learn that games are usually only successful when everyone adheres to the rules but there are also differing versions and perspectives. They learn that they have choices and that others will listen to their ideas.

Research indicates that some childhood games are culturally specific while others can be found in various forms across different cultures. Interestingly, a study carried out by Roberts and Sutton-Smith in 1962 found evidence of an association between the type of games played (whether they were predominantly based on strategy, skill or luck) and the type of upbringing of different groups of children (where the emphasis was placed on responsibility, achievement or obedience). Whatever the main orientation of games might be, the role played by parents and carers (and often by the wider family network) in supporting a child's emotional development is of course tremendously important. The special time shared during a fun game can be a boost to helping family members to understand each other, show their love, and strengthen their relationship. Sharing moments of laughter, problem-solving and creativity during games can be rewarding and re-affirming for everyone concerned.

In games, children who have difficulty in understanding and expressing their feelings verbally, can begin to explore difficult emotions in safety and with the spirit of 'play'. In this way, games help in the process of reflection and demonstrate to children that they are not alone in their feelings and that others have things in common with them. This aspect of games can easily be enhanced through careful facilitation by an adult.

Of course, games alone are not the panacea for all emotional ills and there is no single method or game that can be guaranteed to appeal to all children or to consistently help to solve particular problems or ensure certain responses. However, they are undoubtedly an important part of a child's development. Without this awareness on our part, the many opportunities for helping children to build physical, cognitive, social, and emotional skills through the medium of games can so easily be missed, or worse still, we may unwittingly foster feelings of low self-esteem in children and trigger uncomfortably intense or inappropriate emotional responses.

Games reflect aspects of real life. The ways in which children engage in them often reflects their approach to life in general.

As mindful facilitators of the game process, we can make certain hypotheses about the way that children participate in structured games. First, the way a child acts and reacts in a game situation is likely to reflect her life experiences in some way and therefore also reflect how she behaves in other situations. So, without being overly analytical or too literal in our interpretations of children's behaviour during play it is never the less important for us to be aware of general patterns. Are there children who take a long time to warm up to each game? Are there some who are 'taking over'? What happens when children become frustrated or cannot tolerate waiting their turn? Are they able to recognize personal achievements and those of others? Do they behave independently or always look to others to take the lead? Are they able to take on different roles at different times or for different types of game?

A second hypothesis that we might make centres on children's capacity for change. Working within a humanistic framework, we can approach the playing of games with the assumption that all children, whatever their current abilities, have within them the resources, and therefore the potential, for change and growth. However small or large the changes might be, the ability to respond with a degree of flexibility in different situations and the ability to learn from active participation is part of what it is to be human.

Finally, we should also remember that each child's attitude to different games, his degree of participation and his enjoyment of the game will change over time as he matures and learns.

Games provide valuable learning opportunities in many different areas of social and personal development.

I like David Cohen's exclamation 'Ponder the irony! Children are the experts at play, play is their work and yet we, long-out-of-practice oldies, think we can teach them how to play!' (Cohen 1993, p.13) and Vivian Paley's expansion on this: 'We were taught to say that play is the work of children. But watching and listening to them, I saw that play was nothing less than Truth and Life' (Paley 1991, p.17).

Games not only provide a means to address issues that have already been identified as causing some difficulties but can also be played in a pro-active way to prevent future problems from occurring. In the context of this book, they can be viewed as providing steps towards building and maintaining successful anger management strategies; steps that need to be continually repeated and reinforced in order to have maximum effect.

Figure 3.1 gives an indication of just some of the many specific and more general learning opportunities available to children through structured games sessions.

Undoubtedly, there are many more aspects that could be added according to the orientation of the group (family group, class, occupational therapy group, speech and language therapy group, after school group etc). The following chapter explores issues specifically related to working with groups and in particular to the responsibility of adults in regard to structuring the emotional environment.

Specific learning/consolidation of skills

Developing spoken language skills

Developing listening skills

Developing observation skills

Ability to follow complex instructions

Ability to be reflective

Developing memory skills

Ability to give instructions

Creating new rules and conventions

Ability to take turns and tolerate waiting

Developing problem-solving skills

Ability to cooperate with group members

Developing self-responsibility and leadership skills

Building the ability to persist with an activity

Making mistakes in a safe environment

Ability to acknowledge others' actions and give feedback

Development of body image and body awareness

Understanding the different functions of games

Understanding and exploring different types of games

Using communication skills appropriately for context

Developing ability to select and modify games and rules appropriately

Learning through 'doing' not 'producing'

Exploring social and cultural aspects of games

Learning how games can reinforce previous learning

Recognizing that learning can span several subjects at once

Promoting the idea that learning is fun

Understanding rules that are made by someone else

Understanding how rules are made

Personal/social learning

Process learning

Building self-respect and respect of others

Understanding concepts of tolerance, fairness and empathy

Understanding concept of responsibility for own actions and how behaviour affects others

Recognizing and understanding emotions

Tolerating frustration and building emotional resilience

Reducing impulsivity and building persistence

Exploring links between thoughts, actions and feelings

Developing sensitivity to other people's strengths and difficulties

Building confidence

Building self-efficacy

Extending conscious awareness

Exploring self-concept

Building trust

Learning about the *social* value of individual achievements

Learning to be flexible in thought and action

Thinking independently and imaginatively

Transferable skills

Changes in attitudes or beliefs as result of learning from the social context of games

Reaching an understanding of complex experiences through a non-threatening medium

Devising own games as a result of understanding the general rules about the structure and content of games

Non-specific learning/consolidation of skills

Figure 3.1 Learning opportunities available to children through structured games

Structuring the emotional environment

Key points

- The core conditions of
empathy, unconditional
positive regard and congruence
proposed by Carl Rogers offer
an important framework for
supporting anger management.

- Roles, rules and boundaries
need to be clearly defined so
that children feel safe.

- A nurturing environment is one
in which all emotions are
acknowledged and valued.

- Praise is most effective when it
is specific and realistic.

- A solution-focused approach
helps children to recognize
their skills, strengths and resources.

When children are in groups together, they will all have feelings about the feelings of the other children! Displays of anxiety or anger by one child may trigger feelings of anxiety, anger or distress in another. It will be the facilitator's task to help children to regulate their emotions within the group and demonstrate a calm way of reacting to any displays of strong emotion (see Chapter 5: When a child is already angry, pages 43–46).

The core conditions of empathy, unconditional positive regard and congruence
proposed by Carl Rogers offer an important framework for supporting
anger management.

In order to facilitate a safe and supportive atmosphere for game playing, the three core conditions for supportive relationships proposed by Carl Rogers are useful concepts to keep in mind. These core conditions are empathy, unconditional positive regard and congruence.

Empathy

Empathy is a term freely used but often misunderstood. Roger's own definition highlights the profound and powerful nature of an empathic relationship:

> It means entering the private perceptual world of the other and becoming thoroughly at home in it. It involves being sensitive, moment by moment, to the changing felt meanings which flow in this other person, to the fear or rage or tenderness or confusion or whatever that he or she is experiencing. It means temporarily living the other's life, moving about in it delicately without making judgements; it means sensing meanings of which he or she is scarcely aware, but not trying to uncover totally unconscious feelings since this would be too threatening… It means frequently checking with the person as to the accuracy of your sensing, and being guided by the responses you receive. (Rogers 1980, quoted in Hargarden and Sills 2002, p.35)

As already emphasized, empathy is a vital element in healthy anger management too. Specific games have been included to help children to develop the ability to empathize with others.

Unconditional positive regard

Unconditional positive regard refers to the helper's attitude towards the other person. It is an attitude of valuing the other person for who they are – an 'outgoing positive feeling without reservations, without evaluations' (Rogers 1961, p.62). This can be conveyed to children in the simplest of ways. For example, by making sure that you have acknowledged each child in the group by name as they arrive, and by giving some indication that you are glad they are there (a smile, a 'thumbs up' gesture etc.).

Congruency

Congruency refers to the way in which the helper or facilitator is aware of his own feelings and attitudes and remains true to them. Rogers suggested that congruency engenders a sense of trust in the other person because they feel that they are with someone who is genuine.

In practical terms facilitators can demonstrate these core conditions in a number of ways. The following areas should all be given careful consideration:

- roles, rules and boundaries
- understanding and valuing emotions
- praising
- self-reflection.

Self-reflection is covered in Chapter 6. The next section looks at each of the other three elements in turn and explores them in relation to playing games in groups. However, although the focus is on group interactions, the principles apply just as much to playing games with individual children or within families.

Roles, rules and boundaries need to be clearly defined so that children feel safe.

Formulating ground rules for groups who are specifically working on anger manage-ment is obviously particularly important in order to ensure that the group is a safe place to be. For some children, new games can be scary and we need to spend time building trust amongst group members and between ourselves and the children we are supporting. Trust is most easily established if roles, rules and boundaries are clearly outlined at the start of a group. This can help children to feel 'contained' and safe. An example of a clear time boundary might be: 'Today the games session will be 10 minutes long and when we have finished the game we will do X', or 'every morning we will play one game during circle time and then we will...'

It is also the facilitator's task to set the tone of the games and to demonstrate a firm but fair approach to prevent difficulties arising, for example from children being consistently very dominant or ridiculed by others because they do not understand the game rules. It is crucial that all group members (including family groups) under-stand the importance of supporting each other's participation – even games that purport to be non-competitive can sometimes be played in a competitive, even aggressive way unless there are clear guidelines. Again, this will enable the children to feel safe within the structure of the games and allow them the opportunity to experiment and explore; to expand their self-concept and to self-evaluate without fear of being judged harshly.

Because of the multi-faceted nature of games there will be multiple roles for those who choose to coordinate games sessions with young children. It is important to decide which roles you are taking on. Although these may change and evolve over time, deciding on your role and the purpose of the games you choose will help you to structure and reflect on the sessions more effectively. Possible roles might include several of the following at any one time:

- role model
- teacher/provider of challenges
- facilitator/encourager/enabler
- supporter/helper
- mediator/arbitrator
- observer
- participant
- researcher/information gatherer/assessor
- supervisor
- provider of fun
- ideas person
- time keeper.

Consider whether or not the roles you are taking on conflict in any way and if so, which one you need to concentrate on. Perhaps a second person is needed to take a different perspective or role? For example, can you be facilitator/encourager and also record information about how individuals are coping with different aspects of a particular game?

In which role are you happiest? Do you feel most comfortable as 'provider of fun' or most comfortable in the 'teaching' role?

What about the roles of the children? These too may change and evolve over time so that group members each have the opportunity to be the game coordinator or the 'ideas' person or 'teacher'. Those who feel unable to join in with a particular game may enjoy being timekeeper or observer. Children who understand the rules of games and can explain these to others may naturally take on the role of arbitrator or game coordinator, leading others in making choices and in ensuring that the rules are understood and followed by all participants. This is a valuable skill which can be facilitated during many of the games suggested in this book.

Monitoring of games by the participants themselves is an important aspect of play. Children who would normally find this role difficult can be gradually encouraged and supported in leading and monitoring fairly. Those children who have plenty of experience in arbitrating and leading games can also be encouraged to support this process by stepping back to allow others to have a go.

Games sessions also need 'rules' or guidelines to help foster the feeling of trust and safety among those taking part. Two of the most important rules for facilitators to make clear are:

1. *Children will always be given the choice of staying in or out of the game.* For children who opt out frequently you may want to suggest an alternative role such as timekeeper to encourage some initial involvement. For some anxious children, observing others engaging in a game without feeling in any way included could allow the build up of negative emotions, whereas for others it gives them the opportunity to prepare themselves to join in by watching what happens and familiarizing themselves with the rules.

2. *Children who are reluctant to take part straight away may choose to join in at any time by giving a signal.*

A nurturing environment is one in which all emotions are acknowledged and valued.
How do we help children to be constructively aware of their emotions? The key is to acknowledge and validate feelings. For example, if a child with a hearing difficulty says 'I hate this game, it's stupid', think about the feeling behind the comment. Avoid interpretations but comment on what you see, hear and feel. Aim to support rather than rescue. Responses such as 'But everyone else is enjoying it, I'm sure you will too', 'You haven't tried it yet, let's have a go together' or 'That's OK, you can sit this one out if you like' would probably all get a negative reaction. But making a hypothesis about the feeling behind the words and making an appropriate comment ('It's a very noisy game and I noticed that it's hard to hear the instructions sometimes. I wonder if it would be more fun for you to stand nearer the teacher') can help the child to feel understood and is more likely to lead to him making adjustments in his self-evaluation.

If children become restless do not insist on continuing for a certain number of set rounds of a game, take it as an indication that it is not the right time or not the right game for this group. Children's comments about a game may also point you in the direction of another game to address that particular issue.

Praise is most effective when it is specific and realistic.
Praise and demonstration of pleasure in a child's abilities, perseverance, sense of fun etc. can be an excellent motivator for continued change and development but it will be of little value if it is not genuine or has no personal meaning for the child. If praise does not resonate with his self-concept and self-evaluations he is very likely to reject it. Also, unrealistic or unjustified praise could set him up for experiencing low self-esteem if he tries to do things before he is ready or if it leads to him developing

unrealistically high expectations of what he can achieve. Unfortunately, even when adults do offer genuine praise this can so frequently be followed by a qualification of some sort, negating the praise completely. Such qualified praise might go something like:

'What a great way to share – if only you'd done that this morning you wouldn't have got into a fight!'

'Well done for sticking to the rules – why can't you always do that without getting grumpy?'

'I noticed that you were being really helpful when Sam was upset – you'd usually get cross with him wouldn't you?'

Similarly, it can be all too easy to offer praise that indicates the lesser achievements of others. An award for the fastest worker or best listener for example, suggests that there are others in the group who are not so good at this and also gives little scope for further development (if I am already the best, I don't need to think about that any more!).

The most effective approach is to use genuine specific, descriptive praise whenever possible: 'I liked the way you really listened to what Josh had to say about following the rules of the game', 'I noticed you were being very helpful when Sam got upset and that really worked because he calmed down straight away!'

Sometimes it is also helpful to acknowledge difficulties and empathize with the feelings: 'It looked like it was hard for you to wait your turn. You had lots of great ideas to share! That must have been really frustrating for you!'

Model and encourage realistic, positive praise: 'What did you like about the way that Josh handled that?' Encourage older children to reflect on what happens within games, picking up on the encounters and strategies that are working well and in particular any moments of difficulty which have been successfully negotiated. Use memory aids if necessary to remember what children have done in previous games sessions. Non-judgemental comments on past experiences and actions can be extremely motivating and self-affirming for children.

Non-verbal signals of approval and encouragement can also be very effective. A 'thumbs up', a wink or a smile across a room can all indicate to a child that you have noticed them without drawing the attention of other children in the group – this sort of 'private' praise is particularly helpful for children who are anxious and may be enough to break the train of thought that could lead to frustration and anger.

Christine Durham, in her book *Chasing Ideas* (Durham 2006) describes a great way to make praise a fun interaction. She suggests the use of acronyms and abbreviations such as VIP (very important proposition) or IT (insightful thinking). For older children, this could start as a game in itself – perhaps taking familiar acronyms and familiar sayings and encouraging group members to make up 'secret' messages about behaviour and thoughts that are specific to anger management. For example VIP could be 'Very Imaginative Problem-Solver' or ACE could be 'A Cool Example'. Giving a child a 'thumbs up' sign and saying 'ACE' then becomes even more mean-ingful and fun!

A solution-focused approach helps children to recognize their skills, strengths and resources.

When children are having difficulty in changing habitual anger patterns, engaging them in solution-focused strategies can be extremely useful. Solution-focused brief therapy is a recognized therapeutic approach, widely used to facilitate change in a variety of contexts. As its name suggests, this approach encourages solution-based, rather than problem-based dialogue. Some of the basic assumptions and styles of interaction inherent in this approach are easily incorporated into daily contacts with children and can make a big difference to how a child begins to see themselves and the possibility of change.

In essence, solution-focused communication arises quite naturally from a philos-ophy that emphasizes the skills, strengths and resources of individuals. If we believe that a child is capable of change, that they have the resources for change and they don't always need to be told what to do, then our communications will reflect this. Solution-focused language also reflects the assumption that the child will already be doing something that will help him towards his goal, however small that step might be. A sample interaction might go something like this:

Child: I hate these games.

Adult: Sometimes you really hate the games we're playing.

Child: Yeah. No one ever listens to me (kicks the table leg).

(The use of words like 'never', 'always' and 'no one' adds justification to the anger: if no one ever takes any notice of me then I am justified in feeling angry.)

Adult: Some people don't listen to you and then you get angry.

(Anger is acknowledged and deliberately linked with a particular trigger in order to suggest an alternative to the sense of constant anger.)

Child: Yeah!

Adult: So when we're playing these games and you're not angry, how does that feel?

(This introduces the idea of the exception to the rule.)

Child: Dunno. OK I guess.

Adult: You feel OK sometimes. I wonder what will be different when you are feeling OK in the games more often?

(This assumes that the change will happen and helps the child to begin to 'flesh out' the details of what that will be like. The more details 'the preferred future' can be given, the more likely it is to happen.)

In this much shortened version of a possible interaction the adult has acknowledged the problem but has introduced the possibility for change by using words like 'sometimes' and by looking for the exception to the feeling of constant anger. It is important for the child to focus on what they *will* be feeling, doing or thinking not on what they *don't* want. Other questions might therefore include:

What else will you notice?

How will your teacher/classmates know that you are feeling OK?

What will happen then?

A solution-focused approach fits very comfortably with the use of imagery for helping children to talk about things in a way that is one step removed from the painful experiences or difficulties they are facing. For example an adult can offer images if it seems appropriate – 'When you were really angry with Sam just now, I got this image of a tiger that had been hurt. Is that how you felt?' or 'This problem seems like a huge lump of rock to me – we just can't seem to shift it. What could we do about this rock?' Children are often more than willing to put you right and to suggest their own images if they think you haven't quite grasped the essence of what they are feeling: 'No, it's more like a big swampy puddle…!' Simply talking about images in this way can often enable a child to see solutions or can precipitate a shift in perception where none seemed possible before (Plummer 2007).

5

When a child is already angry

Key points

- Children need to know that they can feel angry and still be loved. Adults need to show that they can cope with a child's angry feelings in a calm way.

- 'Time out' is effective if it is carefully structured to give the child time to self-calm.

- Healthy anger management and healthy self-esteem are closely linked.

Children need to know that they can feel angry and still be loved. Adults need to show that they can cope with a child's angry feelings in a calm way.

Having looked at some of the ways in which we can support children in exploring and understanding their emotions, we must also acknowledge that there will be times when we are confronted by an angry child who needs our help 'in the moment'. Ideally we want to offer this before his emotions get out of control. The following strategies can all be used to help a child to cope with his anger in its early stages.

- Stay calm yourself.

- Make sure that you are on the same physical level as him and show that you can handle his anger calmly. If angry feelings are frightening for a child it will be helpful for him to see that you are not fazed by strong emotions yourself and that you will not ignore his need for attention. Ignoring genuine anger may add fuel to the original feelings of anxiety or frustration and trigger further distress.

- Draw on your own empathy skills – how might the child be feeling? What is it that he wants from you?

- Acknowledge the child's distress. It may seem obvious to say 'I can see you're angry' but this also confirms that you have noted his distress and that you take it seriously.

- Younger children may respond well to a hug or gentle stroking from a parent or to having a familiar adult sit down calmly beside them.

- Most children will want to tell you what they are angry about. If this is the case, indicate to the child that you are trying to understand. This could be conveyed by measured repetition of a simple phrase such as 'I'm listening' and/or through your posture and eye contact.

- When the child is able to tell you about his anger give him plenty of time to give you the whole story. Avoid any temptation to rescue the situation or give advice. Talking about anger in this way takes some of the power out of it and means that children are much less likely to act on their anger in inappropriate ways.

- Make sure that you have understood the situation from the child's perspective. Ask him to make plain anything that you have not understood. This will help him to make things clearer in his own mind as well.

- When he has calmed down enough for reasoned discussion, help him to work out what is the best thing to do. Ask what you can do to help or, for younger children, suggest a simple choice.

- Younger children often benefit from help in directing their attention towards a pleasurable activity to soothe their anger. Older children may need the time to engage in an activity that they know will help them to 'cool off' such as going for a walk, reading quietly or listening to music. In a classroom situation a child's energy can be directed into doing something constructive or practical.

- If you know that the child will respond well to humour then this can often defuse the situation very well. However, it is important that the trigger for the anger is first acknowledged and that the child's feeling of anger is respected. Humour should not be used as a way of denying or belittling a genuine emotion.

Most psychologists now agree that encouraging children to act out their anger, for example by shouting at an inanimate object or by punching cushions, is not necessarily a useful strategy for anger management. These actions may in fact be reinforcing unwanted behaviour and do nothing to offer alternative strategies for self-calming.

Where anger has already resulted in unacceptable action such as deliberately breaking an object or entering into conflict with another child:

- Ensure the safety of both the child/children and yourself.

- It is important to make a distinction between the child's feeling of anger and the unacceptable or inappropriate behaviour. Give a clear message about the behaviour first: 'No. We do not accept spitting in this classroom'; 'No. It is not OK to swear at me when you are angry.' Keep your voice calm but firm.

- Having said what is not acceptable, the child needs to know what alternative would be acceptable. This can come immediately or at a later point in the interaction when he is calmer, and is often most effective if he has had some input into formulating a more appropriate response to his anger.

- Whether you give him an alternative immediately or he discusses it with you later, it is vital for an angry child to hear this phrased in positive language. Knowing what not to do doesn't help unless you know what you *can* do instead!

A sensitive adult can usually help children to find a resolution to conflict but it is also important for children to learn how to negotiate and how to sort out their own battles. If an adult always steps in to resolve the situation without teaching the necessary skills then this could simply reinforce the pattern of showing anger instantly and relying on others to deal with it.

Where anger has already resulted in physical harm to another person or damage to property or some other unacceptable outcome it may be appropriate for the child to be involved in helping to put things right. It should be made clear to the child that it is not the feeling of anger that is being addressed but rather the unacceptable or destructive manifestation of that anger. This is most effective where the child has already had prior knowledge of the consequences of such behaviour. The boundaries are clear and the guidelines are being followed. This helps the child to understand that unacceptable behaviour has clear consequences.

'Time out' is effective if it is carefully structured to give the child time to self-calm.
When a child feels flooded with emotion reasoned discussion is likely to be impossible as he will not be able to think logically or take on board what is being said. Giving him 'time out' to allow the body to calm down is usually necessary but it is vitally important to structure this carefully otherwise, rather than giving him time to cool down and to think about his actions, 'time out' can actually fuel the anger:

> a cooling-down period will not work if that time is used to pursue the train of anger-inducing thought, since each such thought is in itself a minor trigger for more cascades of anger. (Goleman 1996, p.63)

If the objective is simply to give the child a chance to calm himself before entering into a rational discussion or before clearing up the damage or apologizing for the hurt, then the time might be more productively spent employing a specific strategy – one which he could possibly use in the future before things get out of hand. Removing himself from the situation and quietly doing something practical to divert his attention from his angry thoughts could do more good for an angry child than spending ten minutes kicking his heels in isolation.

Healthy anger management and healthy self-esteem are closely linked.
In summary, there are several key points to consider when we are helping children to learn healthy anger management strategies. We need to:

- be curious about how he views himself (his theory about who he is)
- be fully aware of how our actions and words affect his self-concept and therefore his feelings of self-worth and competency
- show genuine warmth and respect for him as a unique individual
- show him that he can be upset and angry and still be loved and valued
- help him to develop self-awareness and realization of how his behaviour affects other people
- help him to understand that emotions can change in form and intensity according to many different factors and that this is normal but that it need not be an overwhelming or scary experience
- help him to develop a degree of emotional resilience.

Significantly, these are very similar to the key issues that are involved in supporting the development and maintenance of healthy self-esteem (Plummer 2007).

6

Self-reflection and self-care

Key points

- The reflective process helps us ensure that the support we offer to children is timely and effective.

- If we take care of ourselves we will be more effective as facilitators.

- Games are fun!

The reflective process helps us ensure that the support we offer to children is timely and effective.

The importance of being reflective lies in the way that we use this skill to develop the most effective way of facilitating change in ourselves and in others. In the context of anger management we obviously need to be aware of our own feelings and needs and the way in which what we do and say has a direct effect on the children in our care. You might find the following questions a useful starting point:

- What, if anything, worries me about children's anger?

- How might an angry outburst from a child affect how I feel and behave?

- What triggers my own anger?

- What degrees of anger do I recognize in myself?

- How do I normally express feelings of anger?

- What are my current anger management techniques? Are they successful? How have these been shaped by my past experiences of feeling angry?

- What are my strengths with regard to anger management? What areas could I develop further?

If we take care of ourselves we will be more effective as facilitators.
Most larger groups benefit from having at least two facilitators. It is very difficult to 'hold' a group and to be aware of everything that is going on within and between all the group members if you are working on your own. Having two facilitators gives you the chance to share ideas, keep better track of what is happening and obviously share the responsibility for planning, carrying out and evaluating the sessions.

It is also important for each facilitator to be able to reflect on his or her skills as a group leader and to be able to debrief at the end of each session. This is much harder if you are only able to do this infrequently with a peer or at a scheduled supervision session.

Taking time to reflect on the group process and on the session can enable facilitators to deal with the challenges and joys of a group more effectively and to monitor facilitation skills in ways that are most likely to support the children. An added bonus of course is that constructive discussions with a co-facilitator help to strengthen personal feelings of competency and self-worth.

With regard to the process of games sessions there are also a few areas to think about. The following questions are some that I have found helpful when planning and reviewing sessions:

- What is my role as the game coordinator?
- Why are we playing these particular games? What are my aims/intended outcomes?
- How will I know if I've achieved my aims/outcomes?
- What are my personal feelings about these games?
- Are the games appropriate for the age/cultural background/sex of the children in the group?
- Do I know the 'rules' of the games?
- Who (if anyone) in the group will find the games difficult/challenging/easy?
- Do I need to adapt the games in any way to allow/encourage full participation of all group members?
- What back up strategies will I need?
- How will I handle behaviour that is potentially disruptive to the group?

- Am I aware of why this behaviour might occur?

- If the group is large or diverse in needs do I have a 'support' person available?

- What will I do if a child knows a different version of a game and wants to play that? (For example, you might suggest that you play their version next time or it might be appropriate to share different versions at the time and abandon one of the other games you had planned.)

- Is this the right time for the game(s)?

- Is the room the right temperature?

- Am I feeling up to it?

Games are fun!

After completion of a games session it is useful to take a few moments as soon as you can to reflect on the game(s) you chose to play. What went well? Was there anything that was difficult to monitor? What skills did you use? What did you enjoy about the games? What did the children most enjoy? Remember, reflective practice is not about being judgemental about our own abilities. It is about reflecting on our skills and on our learning and on our ways of navigating any difficulties.

So, the theory finished with, let's get going and *play some games!*

Bibliography

Antidote (2003) *The Emotional Literacy Handbook: Promoting Whole-School Strategies*. London: David Fulton Publishers.

Arnold, A. (1976) *The World Book of Children's Games*. London: Pan Books.

Beswick, C. (2003) *The Little Book of Parachute Play*. Husbands Bosworth: Featherstone Education.

Brandes, D. and Phillips, H. (1979) *Gamesters' Handbook. 140 Games for Teachers and Group Leaders*. London: Hutchinson.

Bruner, J.S., Jolly, A. and Sylva, K. (eds) (1976) *Play: Its Role in Development and Evolution*. Harmondsworth: Penguin.

Eastman, M. and Rozen, S.C. (1994) *Taming the Dragon in Your Child. Solutions for Breaking the Cycle of Family Anger*. New York: John Wiley and Sons.

Eliot, L. (1999) *What's Going on in There? How the Brain and Mind Develop in the First Five Years of Life*. New York: Bantam.

Ellis, M.J. (1973) *Why People Play*. Englewood Cliffs, NJ: Prentice Hall.

Faupel, A., Herrick, E. and Sharp, P. (1998) *Anger Management. A Practical Guide*. Abingdon and New York: David Fulton Publishers.

Goleman, D. (1996) *Emotional Intelligence. Why It Can Matter More than IQ*. London: Bloomsbury.

Gulbenkoglu, H. and Hagiliassis, N. for Scope (Vic.) Ltd. (2006) *Anger Management. An Anger Management Training Package for Individuals with Disabilities*. London and Philadelphia: Jessica Kingsley Publishers.

Johnson, P. and Rae, T. (1999) *Crucial Skills. An Anger Management and Problem Solving Teaching Programme for High School Students*. Bristol: Lucky Duck Publishing.

Liebmann, M. (2004) *Art Therapy for Groups. A Handbook of Themes and Exercises*, (2nd edn). London and New York: Routledge.

Masheder, M. (1989) *Let's Play Together*. London: Green Print.

Neelands, J. (1990) *Structuring Drama Work. A Handbook of Available Forms in Theatre and Drama*. Cambridge: Cambridge University Press.

References

Booker, O. (1999) *Averting Aggression. Safe Work in Services for Adolescents and Young Adults*, (2nd edn). Lyme Regis: Russell House Publishing.

Cohen, D. (1993) *The Development of Play*, (2nd edn). London: Routledge.

Durham, C. (2006) *Chasing Ideas*. London and Philadelphia: Jessica Kingsley Publishers.

Garvey, C. (1977) *Play*. London: Fontana/Open Books.

Gerhardt, S. (2004) *Why Love Matters. How Affection Shapes a Baby's Brain*. London and New York: Routledge.

Gilliom, M., Shaw, D., Beck, J., Schonberg, M. and Lukon, J. (2002) 'Anger regulation in disadvantaged pre-school boys.' *Developmental Psychology 38*, 2, 222.

Goleman, D. (1996) *Emotional Intelligence. Why It Can Matter More than IQ.* London: Bloomsbury.

Hargarden, H. and Sills, C. (2002) *Transactional Analysis. A Relational Perspective*. Hove and New York: Brunner-Routledge.

Harter, S. (1999) *The Construction of the Self*. New York: Guilford Press.

Opie, I. and Opie, P. (1976) Street Games: 'Counting-out and Chasing.' In J.S. Bruner, A. Jolly and K. Sylva (eds) *Play – Its Role in Development and Evolution*. Harmondsworth: Penguin.

Paley, V.G. (1991) *The Boy Who Would be a Helicopter*. London: Harvard University Press.

Plummer, D. (2007) *Helping Children to Build Self-Esteem*, (2nd edn). London and Philadelphia: Jessica Kingsley Publishers.

Renkin, B., Egeland, B., Marvinney, D., Mangelsdorf, S. and Stroufe, A. (1989) 'Early childhood antecedents of aggression and passive withdrawal in early elementary school.' *Journal of Personality 57*, 2.

Roberts, J.M. and Sutton-Smith, B. (1962) 'Child training and game involvement.' *Ethnology 1*, 166–185.

Rogers, C.R. (1961) *On Becoming a Person: A Therapist's View of Psychotherapy*. London: Constable.

Rogers, C.R. (1980) *A Way of Being*. Boston: Houghton Mifflin.

Sunderland, M. (2006) *The Science of Parenting*. London: Dorling Kindersley.

References

Part Two

Games for anger management

As with all games involving the use of equipment, the parachute games outlined in this book should be supervised by an adult at all times. Small children can easily get themselves tangled up in a large parachute – at the very least this can be a very scary experience for them.

Explanatory notes for the adaptation and reflection sections of each game are provided on pages 13–14. The symbols used for each game are also repeated here for ease of reference:

⑤	This gives an indication of the suggested *youngest* age for playing the game. There is no upper age limit.
⏱ 10 mins	An approximate time is given for the length of the game (excluding the discussion time). This will obviously vary according to the size of group and the ability of the players.
🧍🧍🧍	Indicates that the game is suitable for larger groups (eight or more).
🧍🧍	The game is suitable for small groups.
💬💬💬	The game involves a lot of speaking unless it is adapted.
💬💬	A moderate amount of speaking is required by players.
💬	The game is primarily a non-verbal game or one requiring minimal speech.
☑ empathy	This gives an indication of a skill used or developed by playing this game.

7

Non-competitive ways to choose groups and group leaders

It is worth having several different methods of dividing children into groups or pairs or choosing someone to lead a game. For the purpose of these games we want to avoid placing children in a position where they are anxiously waiting to be 'picked' or where the same groups or pairs consistently choose to work together. The following methods are just some of the many ways in which to encourage random selections.

To choose a leader

- Have names in a hat or in separate balloons. Children pick a name or pop a balloon to see who is the leader for that session. This ensures that everyone gets a turn eventually.

- Take turns according to dates of birth (e.g. using just the date in the month).

To choose pairs

- Count round half the circle then start again. The 'one's' work together, 'two's' work together, etc.

- Put two sets of matching objects in a 'lucky dip' box. Children draw out an object and find their partner who has a matching object.

- Children stand in a circle with eyes closed and arms outstretched. They walk across the circle until they meet someone else.

To choose groups

- Sit in a large circle. Count round in sets of two or four or however many small groups are needed. 'One's' then work together, 'two's' work together, etc.

- Count round the circle using colour names, with as many different colours as are needed for the number of groups.

- Deal out playing cards, e.g. all the clubs in one group and diamonds in the other.

8

Warm-ups and ice-breakers

A reminder:

Before you begin to play games with a new group, don't forget to establish the basic ground rules, or play *The rule of the realm* (page 65) to introduce these early on in the session.

What's my name?

⑦
🕐 10 mins
☑ listening	☑ concentration
☑ asking questions	☑ observation
☑ memory	
☑ taking turns	

How to play Players write their name (or how they would like to be known) on a sticky label. They hide the label somewhere on their own clothes, for example in the top of their sock, in a pocket, under their collar or on the sole of their shoe.

Children try to find as many names as possible (within a time limit suitable for the size of the group) without touching anyone. They can only ask questions such as 'Is it on the sole of your shoe?' or 'Can you show me underneath your right foot?' They either write down all the names that they find or try to remember them.

When the time limit is up everyone stands or sits in a circle. The game coordinator stands behind each person in turn and everyone tries to remember that person's name.

Adaptations

⑤

Throw a soft cushion around the group. Each child says her own name when she catches it. After everyone has had a turn, go round again. This time the rest of the group say the name of the child who catches the cushion.

Use a weighted or strangely shaped soft object so that everyone is likely to have some difficulty catching it – a fun way to even out the ability levels in the group.

Put name labels in a bowl. Each child picks out another child's name and tries to find that person in the group and present them with the label.

Make two sets of animal picture labels: one for children to wear and one to put in the bowl. Children pick an animal label from the bowl and find the matching picture worn by a group member.

Reflection What helps you to remember other people's names? What do you feel like when other people remember your name?

Notes

Remember me

⑦
⌚ 10 mins
🧍 🧍
💬

☑ listening
☑ memory
☑ taking turns
☑ concentration

How to play   Players sit in a circle. The first player says her own name. The second player says the first player's name and her own name, the third player says the first two names, and her own name, and so on around the group.

Adaptations   Names are said in time to rhythmic clapping to keep the momentum going.

⑤   Alternate children in the circle take turns to say their own name and the name of the person sitting on their right. This second child claps twice but does not speak. If anyone claps when they should be speaking or speaks when they should be clapping, the whole process changes direction.

Reflection   Is it harder or easier to remember names when you are concentrating on something else as well? Does this apply to other tasks? Does it depend on what the task is?

In later games sessions this could be linked with trying to remember calming strategies when we are feeling angry or frustrated. For example, if I'm trying to fix something and it's hard to do, it will be even harder if I get frustrated but easier if I remember to stay focused and calm.

Notes

Guess the voice

⑦

🕐 10 mins

† † †

🗨

- ☑ listening
- ☑ deduction
- ☑ memory
- ☑ taking turns

- ☑ concentration

How to play
Players stand or sit in a circle. Each player invents a unique vocal call, for example a combination of vowels with different intonation patterns or a hum or a whistle. The whole group listens to each call in turn as the players say their first name and then their chosen sound.

One person stands in the centre of the circle with a blindfold on. The game coordinator silently chooses someone to make their call. The person in the centre tries to name the caller. If they get it right they can have a second turn.

Each person has a maximum of two turns before the coordinator chooses another person to sit in the centre.

Adaptations
⑤
Callers recite one line of a well-known song or a pre-chosen phrase that all the children are able to say/remember.

Two people stand in the centre and can confer about the name of the caller.

The person who was last in the centre can choose the next caller.

Everyone changes seats before the caller is chosen.

The players are split into pairs to practise their calls. One child from each pair then stands in the centre of the circle and is blindfolded. On a signal their partners make their chosen calls. The players who are blindfolded have to carefully move around the circle until they find their partner.

Reflection
How do we recognize individual voices? What makes our voices different? What might happen if we all sounded exactly the same? What words can we use to describe different voices (for example deep, gruff, loud, soft, like chocolate)? Keep these descriptions very general, rather than specific to individual children.

Does your voice change according to how you are feeling?

Notes

Signs and signatures

⑦
🕐 5 mins
♦ ♦ ♦
💬💬

☑ listening
☑ memory
☑ taking turns
☑ concentration

☑ observation
☑ non-verbal
   communication

How to play | Players sit in a circle. The first player says his or her name accompanied by a movement/gesture (e.g. head movement, clapping, making sweeping gesture with both hands). The next child introduces the previous child (using their name and gesture) and then says their own name accompanied by their own gesture.

This is _____ and I am _____

Finish with everyone saying and gesturing their own name at the same time.

Adaptations
⑤
💬

Players say their own name and think of a gesture but do not need to introduce anyone.

Play the game standing up and include large movements such as jump back, shake leg, hop.

Teach the children specific signs, such as finger spelling for their initials or signs for different animals.

In smaller groups players can try and remember the names and gestures of as many previous players as possible (in a similar way to the game *Remember me* on page 59).

Reflection | If you had a different name, would you choose a different gesture? Do you think other people would link this gesture with your name?

Think of a family member or a friend. What gesture might they choose to go with their name? Would you choose a different gesture for them or the same one?

Does the gesture reflect your personality in some way? Talk about the differences and similarities in how you see yourself and how you think others see you.

Notes

Fruit salad

⑤
🕐 5 mins
♀ ♀ ♀
♀

☑ listening
☑ memory
☑ categorization
☑ concentration

☑ observation

This is a fast paced game that can easily be adapted to suit different likes and dislikes. For that reason it can be played many times in different formats and is always a favourite among groups of active children!

How to play   Sit in a circle with one person standing in the centre. Each person chooses the name of a different fruit. The person in the centre calls out two fruits. These two children swap places and the caller tries to sit in one of their seats before the other person gets there. If the caller says 'fruit salad' everyone swaps seats! The person left standing is the next caller.

Adaptations   Swap chairs if you have something in common, e.g. had cereal for breakfast this morning, have brown eyes. Everyone swaps when the caller says something that he knows everyone has in common.

Motorway – using car names

Zoo-keeper – using animal names

And anything else that comes in groups!

For larger groups and the younger age range have a limited number of items so that there is more than one child for each one (four apples, four bananas etc). This can get quite hectic with lots of children running across the circle at the same time so take care!

Reflection   Do different children like different versions? Why?

Why can some games be frustrating for some players?

What do all games have in common?

⑩   Debate the pros and cons of competitive games and cooperative games.

Notes

Circle move

⑤

⏱ 5 mins

👤 👤 👤

💬

☑ self-awareness
☑ eye contact
☑ taking turns
☑ concentration

☑ observation

How to play   Players sit in a circle. One child starts off a movement such as a shoulder shake. Each child copies this in turn until everyone is making the same movement. Then everyone stops in turn until the circle is still. The person sitting to the left of the first player then starts a different movement and sends this around the group in the same way. Do this as many times as feels comfortable, varying the speed.

Adaptations   Two players sitting on opposite sides of the circle start off two different movements at the same time and send them in the same direction or in opposite directions.

Players 'throw' the movement to each other across the circle by gaining eye contact with another player.

Reflection   How does keeping eye contact help you to feel confident?

Why is it helpful to be aware of our own body language and that of others?

Notes

Magic threes

⑦
🕐 10 mins
❖ ❖
ᗡᗡᗡ

☑ trust
☑ listening
☑ memory
☑ taking turns

☑ concentration

How to play	Players have three minutes to walk around the room and introduce themselves to three other people. Each child tells these three people three important facts about themselves. For younger children this could be full name, something I hate and something I like. For older children this could be my greatest achievement, my best birthday and my most treasured possession, or one thing that makes me angry, one thing I do to 'chill out' and one thing I want to achieve.
	When the time is up, everyone sits in a circle and recounts as much information about as many other children as possible.
Adaptations	Pairs share the information and then introduce each other to the rest of the group.
	Players divide into groups of three or four and try to find three things that they all have in common. One person from each small group tells the whole group what these three things were.
Reflection	How difficult or easy was it to remember what you heard? What would make it easier/harder to remember facts about other people? Why is it important to remember what people tell us about themselves? What does it feel like when someone remembers something important about you? What does it feel like when people get the facts wrong?
	What does it feel like to know that you have things in common with other people? Was it difficult or easy to find things in common?
Notes	

The rule of the realm

⑦
🕐 10 mins
† † †
ᏇᏇᏇ

☑ listening
☑ cooperation
☑ memory
☑ deduction

☑ problem-solving
☑ observation

This game encourages players to work together in order to solve a puzzle about group rules.

How to play Divide the group into two. Group A leaves the room. Group B makes up a 'talking rule' such as 'every time you speak you must cross your arms' or 'every time you finish speaking you must scratch your head'. The game coordinator checks that everyone in group B remembers to do this by asking each one a simple question such as 'Do you like chocolate?' or 'How old are you?' Group A returns to the room and the coordinator repeats the previous questions or asks similar ones while group A observe. The aim is for group A to guess the rule. The emphasis is on group problem-solving – if one person in group A guesses the correct rule, this means that the whole group have achieved. Older children can therefore be encouraged to confer before they guess the rule.

Adaptations Allow a maximum of five guesses.

Rules for older and very able children can be quite complex such as 'when the coordinator asks you a question it is the person on your left who answers' or 'you have to use the last word from the question to start your answer'.

All the group stay in the room and the coordinator chooses a place to set up his or her kingdom e.g. 'the moon', the 'playground'. Each person says what they will bring if they are chosen to be part of the new kingdom. The rule that they have to discover either relates to the first letter of their own name or relates to the first letter of the place where the kingdom will be. The coordinator starts by giving a few examples such as 'Sandip would be welcome in the new kingdom if he brought snakes with him but not if he brought money. Miriam would be welcome if she brought money, but definitely not if she brought jewels'. The coordinator tells group members if they can join the kingdom or not according to what they offer to bring with them. This needs a strict time limit and therefore clues may need to be made more and more obvious to give everyone the chance to guess the 'rule' and join the kingdom. Children should be encouraged to help each other out towards the end of the game in order to ensure that no one is left out.

Reflection   Do all groups need rules? Why/why not? Are some rules more useful than others?

               What does it feel like to not know a group rule when it seems like everyone else knows it? What should groups do about that?

               What should the rules be for this group?

               What do you think about having rules for anger? Should there be rules about how people show anger, or does it depend on the situation?

Notes

Additional notes: more ideas for warm-ups and ice-breakers

Reflections

9

Lighting the fuse: exploring anger and triggers to anger

Emotion masks

⑥
🕐 5 mins
♟ ♟ ♟
💬

☑ self-awareness
☑ imagination
☑ non-verbal
  communication

☑ dramatic
  awareness
☑ turn-taking
☑ observation

How to play   Players sit in a circle. The first player 'pulls a face' to show a strong emotion, then 'removes' the face with their hands as if it were a mask and passes it to the player on their left. This player 'puts on' the mask, copying the expression as accurately as possible. The second player then changes the expression and passes it on to the next person and so on around the circle.

Adaptations
⑤   Introduce a limited number of options to pass around the circle, e.g. happy, sad and angry. Get all the children to practise these first.

⑦   Limit the part of the mask that can be altered, e.g. only the eyes and eyebrows, or just the mouth.

Reflection   Which masks did players think they were putting on? What emotions did players pass to others? Did these match up? Is it possible to show an emotion with just one part of the face? Were there different degrees of any similar emotions passed around? How do we show different degrees of emotion (e.g. by facial expression, posture, actions)?

Talk about how we can have different levels of the same feeling in different situations – like having a volume control or an intensity control – for example, we could be slightly frustrated when we make a mistake and furious when someone accuses us of something that we didn't do.

Anger is just one of many normal emotions. Anger can be felt at different levels. Think of as many words as possible to describe different levels of anger.

Notes

Emotions

⑤
⏱ 5 mins
👤 👤 👤
💬

☑ self-awareness
☑ non-verbal
   communication
☑ imagination

☑ dramatic
   awareness

How to play   The game coordinator suggests different emotions and all members of the group try to show these emotions in any non-verbal way they like, for example as an animal, as a movement, by facial expression or the way they walk. The coordinator shouts 'freeze' and everyone 'holds' the pose and feels what it's like for a few seconds.

Shake that feeling out of the body (shake arms, hands, legs). Then try a different emotion. Finish with at least two positive emotions.

Adaptation   Act out actions and feelings together randomly e.g. doing the ironing sadly, eating a sandwich angrily.

Reflection   Sometimes we can be saying one thing and feeling something completely different. Does our body language sometimes 'give the game away'? If someone tells you they are angry but they are smiling would you believe their words or their facial expression?

How do you usually show that you are angry? How do you usually show that you are happy or sad?

Notes

What does anger feel like?

⑧
🕐 **60 mins**
👤 👤 👤
💬

☑ self-awareness
☑ creative thinking
☑ understanding
   metaphors

☑ concentration
☑ observation

This requires some preparation by the game coordinator beforehand

How to play   Divide the group into two halves. Groups A and B then work in different rooms or in different parts of the same room but must not look at what the other group is doing. Within each group children work in pairs or threes to draw round each other's body outline on large pieces of paper. Each child uses pictures from comics, catalogues, magazines etc. to 'clothe' their body outline with shapes and colours or objects to represent how his or her body feels when they experience anger.

Group A try to guess who each of the pictures belong to in group B and vice versa.

Adaptations   Once clothed, add words, headlines and catchphrases to represent useful and
⑩   not useful aspects of anger.

Players pick emotion cards from a selection provided by the game coordinator and make their body pictures according to the chosen emotion. Everyone tries to guess the emotion portrayed.

Make a joint picture, each player adding a different physical symptom of anger.

Reflection   When you look at all the figures can you see anything that any of them have in common? What are the main differences?

When is anger useful? What other feelings might cause similar sensations in your body (e.g. a knotted stomach could be excitement, clenched fists could be linked with determination)?

Notes

Living links

⑧
⏱ 10 mins
♦ ♦ ♦
♡

☑ self-awareness   ☑ observation
☑ listening
☑ taking turns
☑ concentration

How to play   Players stand in a circle. The game coordinator chooses someone to start off a living link. This person calls out something that makes him feel angry. Anyone who feels angry for the same reason, holds hands with the first person and then calls out a different trigger to anger. When several players respond at the same time, it is the last person in the chain who calls out the next link. This continues until all players are connected. If the whole group connects after only two or three triggers have been named players can break and regroup, starting with a new caller.

While players are still holding hands, talk briefly about anger as a chain reaction, triggered by an event and a thought.

Invite the children to dissolve the anger chain by slowly letting go of each other's hands. Get everyone to shake their arms, hands, shoulders and legs.

Adaptations   Stay seated in the circle and use string to connect players instead of holding hands.

The game coordinator calls out groupings in quick succession and everyone has to group and regroup as fast as they can, according to the category.

Reflection   Talk about the similarities and differences in triggers to anger. What happens if someone is angry for several different reasons? Talk about the strength of the anger chain. When might this be a very positive aspect of anger? When might it lead to problems?

Notes

Pass the message

⑤

🕐 10 mins

♦ ♦ ♦

Qꞯ

☑ listening
☑ taking turns
☑ concentration
☑ waiting

This well known 'Whispers' game is a fun way of demonstrating how what we say can be misinterpreted or distorted. It also promotes tolerance of mild frustration.

How to play

Players are seated in a circle. Player One whispers a short sentence to the next person in the circle, who whispers it to the next person and so on until it gets back to Player One again. The final sentence heard is then compared to the original version.

Adaptations

Player One draws a simple shape or picture with one finger on the back of Player Two who has to pass it on around the circle.

Player One draws a simple picture on a piece of paper then shows it briefly to Player Two who has to draw it from memory before showing the new version to Player Three and so on.

Reflection

Talk about how facts can be distorted and how rumours can be spread. Compare the different versions of the pictures or the spoken sentences. Is it easy or difficult to remember the details of what we see and hear? Talk about how things we say and do can be remembered inaccurately. What should we do if we think someone is spreading false rumours about us or has been given wrong information about us?

Notes

Cartoons

⑩
🕐 **45 mins**
🯅 🯅 🯅
🗨🗨🗨

☑ cooperation
☑ making judgements
☑ negotiation

☑ understanding stereotypes

How to play
Players divide into small groups. Each group collaborates to make a cartoon or a collage of a scene depicting some sort of conflict or a situation where at least one person is feeling angry. Groups then share their cartoons and try to guess what each other's pictures represent.

Adaptation
Players divide into small groups and devise a one minute silent play, depicting a scene of conflict or a situation where at least one person is angry. They then act out their plays for the rest of the group to guess the situation.

Reflection
Talk about differing viewpoints and different interpretations of the pictures and plays. Was there any indication of bias or stereotyping? How are these relevant to feelings of anger and to anger management?

Notes

Additional notes: more ideas for exploring anger and triggers to anger

Reflections

When I'm angry:
responses and consequences

Waves on the sea parachute game

⑤

⌚ 10 mins

👤 👤 👤

💬

☑ listening
☑ co-ordination
☑ concentration
☑ imagination

With a little imagination, many games can be adapted to include the use of a parachute. Parachute games are fun for children of all ages and provide an excellent focus for outdoor play.

How to play   Children stand in a circle, holding the parachute with both hands at waist level. A large soft ball is placed in the middle of the parachute. The game coordinator gives instructions for how calm or stormy the waves on the 'sea' should be and the children move the parachute accordingly, while trying to stop the soft ball from falling off.

Finish with a calm rippling of the parachute and gently lay it on the ground. All the children sit quietly around the outside of the 'sea'. For young children this would be a good time to tell a story that has a sea theme. Older children could make up a sea story, each adding one sentence in turn.

Adaptations   Tell the story of a land storm brewing, from gentle rain to a tornado and then subsiding again. The children move the parachute according to the different stages of the storm.

Have several soft balls on the parachute at the same time.

Players take turns to give instructions for moving the parachute in different ways at ground level (e.g. like ripples on a pond, like great waves, like a sheet of ice) while two or more players walk across the surface in an appropriate way to match the motion.

Reflection   Difficult emotions can build and subside or can come on very suddenly and perhaps unexpectedly. Pleasant emotions come and go as well. This is normal.

What happened to the soft balls when the sea was raging or the tornado was strong?

How did group members feel when they were trying to keep the soft balls on the parachute at different stages of the storm? What happens if our angry emotions get out of control? How might this affect us? How might it affect other people around us?

Notes

How many feelings?

⑦
🕐 30 mins
† † †
ᗑᗑᗑ

☑ empathy
☑ cooperation
☑ categorization
☑ negotiation

☑ trust

This game is about recognizing other people's feelings and noting similarities in feelings. It also helps children to recognize different degrees of emotion. You will need to make enough large wall charts for the number of groups playing plus one extra. Each chart should have four giant ladders drawn on it – one for each emotional theme.

How to play   Groups are given a time limit in which to think of as many feeling words as possible within the four themes of anger, fear, sadness and joy. Each word is written on separate cards. Players in each group then decide between themselves where each emotion word should be placed on the ladders. For example 'furious' and 'annoyed' would be placed on the anger ladder but annoyed would be near the bottom of the ladder and furious would be higher up. Groups then combine to negotiate making a final wall chart to show all the emotions in an agreed order.

Adaptation   Mark out a long line on the floor to indicate a scale of one to ten. Groups of children choose a category and then each pick one of the emotion words from that category. They then arrange themselves in order of intensity along the line.

Reflection   Were there any disagreements about levels of emotions? Do some people experience emotions near the top of the ladders a lot of the time? How can we recognize different levels of similar emotions in ourselves and in others? Do we sometimes have a high intensity emotion for low intensity situations?

Notes

Hands up!

⑦
🕐 5 mins
🚶 🚶 🚶
💬

☑ self-awareness
☑ imagination
☑ dramatic
   awareness

☑ non-verbal
   comminucation

The children need to stand in a large enough space so that they have room to move their arms and hands without touching other people.

How to play   Demonstrate how we can move our arms freely in the air and at the same time shake our hands loosely. When all the children are moving freely the game coordinator calls out a word that reflects a degree of anger (e.g. annoyed, frustrated, furious, cross). Players begin an angry conversation between their two hands. After thirty seconds the coordinator calls 'hands up'. Players raise their hands above their heads and stretch as high as they can go. The coordinator then calls another anger word and players drop their arms down and act out another conversation between their hands until the coordinator calls 'hands up' again. Continue for at least four levels of anger then finish with a calm conversation. Instead of 'hands up' at the end, the coordinator calls 'hand shake'. Players shake hands with themselves!

Adaptations   Invent a 'hand dance' changing from calm to angry and back again. In small groups players can take turns to demonstrate their hand dance or to teach it to the rest of the group.

Players work in pairs to have an angry conversation through drawing, making marks and shapes with paint or crayons on the same piece of paper. Each player uses one colour and takes turns to draw their part of the conversation. Players must keep to their own half of the paper. Finish with a resolution and a calming down.

Reflection   Talk about any physical tension evident during the game. Are there times when our hands show how we are feeling? If our hands are tense does anything happen to the rest of our body?

Talk about how even small changes in body tension and posture (e.g. unclenching your jaw or relaxing your hands) can make a big difference to how we feel and to how other people *think* we feel. Can you think of postures that look nearly the same but mean something very different?

How do you stand or sit when you are feeling angry? How do other people know when you are feeling angry? What is the smallest thing that you need to do or to say for other people to know how you are feeling?

If you have an argument or you hit someone or break something in anger are the consequences the same as when you explain to someone why you are feeling angry?

Notes

Just because

⑥
🕐 10 mins

☑ understanding
   cause and effect
☑ listening
☑ concentration
☑ creative thinking

☑ understanding
   opposites
☑ sequencing/
   story-telling

How to play   Player One describes a very simple event such as 'the dog barked'. Player Two gives a reason: 'because it saw a cat'. Player Three gives a possible consequence: 'The postman dropped all the letters'. The next player starts with a new event. Players are encouraged to give the causes and effects as quickly as possible and can be challenged by other players if their answers are not thought to be relevant.

Adaptation
⑧   Play good news and bad news.

Players sit in a circle. The game coordinator starts off with a piece of 'good' news. The next person adds 'but the bad news is…' For example 'the good news is that school is closed for the day…the bad news is that we all have extra homework to do. The good news is that the homework is to write about the local funfair…the bad news is that the funfair is closed for repairs…the good news is that the owner of the funfair is giving away free ice cream…the bad news is they don't have any cones'.

Reflection   Sometimes the outcome of a situation can be very predictable and sometimes it might be quite unexpected. For example, what might be the consequences of breaking something in anger? What could happen if someone is angry because she has been bullied or teased? What will happen if two children have a fight at school? What might happen if you remove yourself from a possible conflict situation?

Talk about being creative in thinking up possible good news related to the 'bad' news. Have you ever been in a difficult situation that turned out to be useful for you?

Notes

Finger puppets

⑤
🕐 20 mins
† † †
💬💬

☑ self-awareness
☑ imagination
☑ planning

☑ sequencing/
   story-telling
☑ dramatic
   awareness

How to play   Each child uses their own unique finger print(s) as a starting point for a drawing or painting of a person. Players cut out their own figures and make up a short puppet show in which the figure tells something about himself or herself to the rest of the group. This does not necessarily have to be directly linked to anger.

Adaptations   Make up a short puppet show in which two figures have difficulty sharing toys but then learn how to share and play together. This could be demonstrated by the game coordinator first and then pairs of children can make up their own one minute puppet shows for the whole group to watch.

Make up puppet shows depicting a variety of situations where frustration, annoyance or anger might be displayed. These feelings could be resolved or unresolved by the end of the performance. The group could then contribute ideas for what the puppets could do next.

Introduce a thumb print puppet as arbitrator or friend.

Reflection   Talk about the uniqueness of finger prints and each of us being unique individuals.

Talk about how we show feelings in different ways and at different levels. What are some of the possible consequences of different levels of anger? Explore the positive aspects of anger when it is expressed appropriately.

What skills did the 'arbitrator' puppet use?

Notes

Guess how!

⑦
🕐 10 mins
🚹 🚹
💬

☑ self-awareness   ☑ deduction
☑ listening
☑ concentration
☑ observation

How to play   Two players leave the room while everyone else decides what 'angry position' or 'calm position' they should take up on their return. For anger this might be something like 'sitting on the floor, facing away from each other with arms and legs folded'. The two players return and try to work out how they should be sitting or standing according to how loudly or quietly the other children are clapping. The closer they get to the target position, the louder the other children clap.

Adaptation   The two children who left the room return and 'arrange' two other children in pre-chosen positions.

Reflection   Sometimes we get feedback from others about whether or not we're succeeding in a task or we're 'on the right track' but sometimes we have to rely on our own self-awareness. Talk about being realistic in self-awareness. How do you know when you are doing something well? How do you know when you are tense or when you are relaxed? How do you know when you need to do something in a different way?

Notes

Consequences

⑩
🕐 10 mins
🧍 🧍
💬

☑ understanding   ☑ sequencing
   cause and effect   ☑ taking turns
☑ imagination
☑ concentration

A familiar party game, adapted to give an emphasis on exploring the consequences of anger.

How to play   Each player starts with a blank strip of paper to write on. The first player writes the name of someone famous (male) at the top of the paper (fictional or real) then folds it down to hide the name. This player passes the paper to his left. The second player writes the word 'met' and adds another famous name (female), folds the paper, and passes it on. The next player writes 'in' or 'at' and adds a place. The next player writes 'He said' and makes up a suitably angry sentence. The next player writes 'She said' and constructs an angry response. The next player writes 'and the consequence was' and writes what happened to them. The last player writes 'The world said' and gives an opinion about the situation. The paper is then passed once more to the left to be read out to the group.

Adaptation   Play the drawing version of this where each player adds a different part of a
⑥   body with the aim of drawing 'an angry person'. The first person draws the head and neck and folds down the paper to leave just the bottom of the neck showing for the next person to add the top part of the body, ending at the elbows and waist and so on.

Reflection   Sometimes anger can be dissolved by humour. When might this be appropriate? When would it not be appropriate? Have you ever felt angry about something that you could laugh about later?

Can you think of a time when something unexpected or funny has happened because someone was angry?

Notes

Additional notes: more ideas for exploring responses and consequences

Reflections

11

You and me: empathy

Silent greetings

⑤

⏱ 10 mins

🧍🧍🧍

💬

☑ empathy

☑ non-verbal communication

☑ memory

☑ concentration

☑ observation

This game requires plenty of space for the children to move around freely.

How to play   Everyone walks slowly around the room, silently greeting each other in a friendly way. For example, a little wave, a long slow wave, offering 'high five', smiling, making eye-contact, having a short 'conversation' between hands. The game coordinator may need to demonstrate a few ideas first. There should be no physical contact during this. The aim is to see how many different ways players can greet each other successfully.

Adaptation   Play a variety of music (e.g. culturally specific music, lively music, slow, gentle music) while the children walk around the room and greet each other in ways that match the different rhythms and themes.

Reflection   Did you learn a new greeting or get a new idea and then try it out on someone else? Did some ways of greeting seem easier than others? What was the most fun/natural/relaxed way to greet others? Which one felt most like 'you'? Did you change your greetings to match other people or did pairs sometimes greet each other in completely different ways? How did that feel?

What are some of the signs that you could look out for to show you that people are thinking about you, or welcoming you into a group, even if they don't say anything (e.g. 'thumbs up', smile)? How might this help you if you are feeling anxious? Can you think of a time when you would be able to give this type of reassurance to someone else?

Notes

Feel it, do it

⑦
🕐 5 mins
👤 👤 👤
💬

☑ empathy
☑ self-awareness
☑ taking turns

☑ dramatic
   awareness
☑ observation

How to play
Players stand in a circle facing each other. Volunteers take turns to take one step into the circle and show with their whole body the way that they are feeling today. Then they say their name (in a way that also reflects the emotion) and step back. The whole group steps forward and reflects back the action and the original person's name. Everyone steps back. The next volunteer steps forward. Players do not need to name the emotions.

Adaptations
Players start by crouching down low. Volunteers 'pop' up (like popcorn!) and then crouch down again when they have shown their feeling and said their name. The whole group 'pops' up to reflect the feeling and then crouches down to wait for the next volunteer.

⑤
The game coordinator suggests a limited number of emotions such as happy, sad and angry. Volunteers 'pop' up to show one of these emotions and everyone else guesses which emotion that person was showing.

Reflection
Do you ever have feelings that you don't understand or don't know why you feel that way? Do people show the same emotions in different ways?

Notes

Mirror talking

⑤
🕐 5 mins
👤 👤 👤
🗨

☑ empathy   ☑ trust
☑ self-awareness   ☑ observation
☑ non-verbal
   communication

How to play   Children sit opposite each other in pairs and take turns to mirror each other's hand movements as closely as possible.

Adaptations   Use music to evoke different moods for the hand movements.

Give a theme beforehand.

Extend to arm movements or whole body movements.

Reflection   How easy or difficult was this? What skills are needed in order to follow someone else's movements in this way? What did you feel when someone else was following your movements?

Notes

Walk this way

⑤   ☑ empathy   ☑ non-verbal
🕐 10 mins   ☑ imagination   communication
🚶 🚶 🚶   ☑ observation   ☑ dramatic
💬   awareness

How to play   The game coordinator asks a 'leader' to walk around the room in a chosen way, e.g. like a giant, like the world's strongest man, or like an older person who has stiff joints. Everyone watches closely and then tries to walk in exactly the same way. When the game coordinator rings a bell or shakes a tambourine everyone 'freezes' in one position. They hold this position for the count of five. Then someone else leads the group in a different type of walk until the coordinator rings the bell again. Continue for at least five different walks.

Adaptations   Walk in different ways to reflect different emotions.

              In pairs try and exactly mirror how your partner walks across the room.

Reflection   Discuss similarities and differences in the way that people walk. Think about 'sameness' and differences in such things as looks, actions, likes and dislikes. What would the world be like if we all talked and moved in exactly the same way? Why would that be difficult? And *then* what would happen? How does it feel to 'walk in someone else's shoes'? How does it feel when someone else really tries to feel what it is like to be you?

Notes

If feelings were colours

⑤
① 10 mins
♦ ♦ ♦
♡

☑ self-awareness
☑ empathy
☑ imagination

☑ non-verbal
   communication
☑ observation

How to play   The game coordinator leads a very brief discussion about how different feelings could be thought of as different colours. For example, 'I'm the colour blue today because I feel calm'; 'I'm the colour blue today because I feel sad'; 'I'm the colour red because I feel full of energy.' Ask the children what colour they would be today and why they would be that colour. The children then try to feel what it is like to move around the room as this colour.

Adaptations   Everyone tries the same colour. Do the movements first and then ask what emotion/feeling the children had when they moved as this colour.

Try three or four different colours in succession.

Groups of children choose a colour to portray to the rest of the group who have to guess which colour it is.

Reflection   Do all the blues move in the same way? How do different colours move? Is it easy to change from one 'mood' to another? When might that happen? What colour is anger? Does anger have different colours according to the intensity of the feeling? Did players choose different colours for the same emotion?

Notes

If he/she were a flower

⑩	☑ empathy	☑ listening
⏱ 10 mins	☑ understanding metaphors	
👤👤	☑ concentration	
🗨🗨		

This game works best when the group members already know a little about each other.

How to play — Players sit in a circle. Player One leaves the room and the others choose someone in the group who will be described. Player One returns to the room and is allowed to ask ten questions in order to find out who the group have chosen. Each question must take the form of 'If this person were a _____ (flower, house, car, bird etc.) what kind of _____ would they be?' When Player One guesses correctly, another person leaves the room and the process is repeated.

Adaptation — Instead of choosing a person, the group chooses an emotion for Player One to guess.

Reflection — We all have many different aspects to our personality. Sometimes the way that other people see us is different to how we see ourselves.

Anger is only one of many emotions that we are capable of experiencing. Feeling angry about specific things is not the same as being an 'angry person'.

Notes

Blind walk

⑧
 🕐 15 mins

☑ empathy
☑ trust
☑ cooperation
☑ listening

☑ supporting
☑ giving instructions

This game requires plenty of space for players to move around in. A few large obstacles can be used for players to negotiate.

How to play   Divide the group into two. One half of the group will act as silent 'protectors' while the other half of the group is led on a blind walk. The protectors will gently prevent the 'explorers' from walking into obstacles or each other (e.g. by touching them on the arm if they get too close). The explorers choose one leader whom they trust to lead them around the room in a snake formation (with the leader as the head of the snake). Each explorer puts one hand on the shoulder of the person in front of them. The game coordinator, the protectors and the line leader all keep their eyes open. The leader can give verbal instructions. Everyone else in the snake has their eyes shut.

Adaptations   Mark out three sides of a large enclosure on the floor. A shepherd tries to round up a group of blindfolded children (sheep) and move them into the pen one at a time using only four words – forwards, backwards, left, right – and a whistle to indicate the number of steps to take.

Players work in pairs and help their partner to 'explore' their surroundings through touch. They can progress from holding their partner's arm to touching an elbow, to just touching finger tips.

Reflection   What did you discover? What helped you to feel safe? Was it the reassurance of the leader? Precise directions? Tone of voice? Did you feel able to ask the leader to slow down if needed? What did it feel like to be the leader? Were you aware of how the rest of the snake was coping with the blind walk? Do you think you gave clear instructions?

Notes

Personal interviews

⑦
🕐 10 mins
👤 👤 👤
💬💬💬

☑ empathy
☑ trust
☑ listening
☑ asking questions

☑ taking turns

How to play
Drape a chair with a brightly coloured blanket or cloth. Children take turns to sit in the chair and are interviewed by the rest of the group. Questions can be about their likes and dislikes, wishes, holidays, favourite books, pet hates, etc. or they can be interviewed about a particular interest they have.

Adaptation
Use two chairs, one for the person being interviewed and one for volunteer interviewers who can come and sit in the chair and ask one question before returning to their place in the audience.

Reflection
How does it feel to have the chance to talk about yourself? How does 'being interviewed' compare to having a conversation with someone? Talk about taking turns in conversations and asking questions to show a genuine interest in the other person. What does it feel like when a friend asks you questions about yourself?

Notes

Additional notes: more ideas for exploring empathy

Reflections

12

You and me together: respect, cooperation and negotiation

Important names

⑦

🕐 5 mins

👤 👤 👤

💬

☑ respecting others
☑ self-awareness
☑ self-respect

☑ understanding characteristics
☑ listening

The ability to cooperate and negotiate is based on self-respect and respect for others.

How to play   Each child chooses a special word to describe herself, beginning with the first letter of her name (e.g. energetic Erin, happy Hilary). Stand in a circle and use a softball or beanbag to throw. On the first round the catcher says her own special name. On the second round the thrower calls out another child's special name as she throws the ball/beanbag to her.

Adaptations   Children choose special names to reflect particular talents (not necessarily using the first letter of their name).

⑤   Use a bell to add a sense of grandeur and dignity to the sound of each name. The first player carries the bell slowly across the circle to another child, trying not to let it ring. The child who receives the bell rings it once and says their special name as the chime resonates around the room (younger children can just say their first name). They then carry the bell across the circle to another child and so on until everyone has had a turn.

Reflection   Think about the enjoyment of saying and hearing your own name. How can you celebrate your name? Take time to reflect on the qualities in yourself that you really like. Why is self-respect important? How do we show self-respect? How do we show respect for others?

Notes

Story-line

⑦
10 mins

☑ self-respect
☑ respect for others
☑ research skills
☑ planning
☑ sequencing/ story-telling

The children will need to do some research at home before this game can be played.

How to play Set children the task of researching their names in preparation for a subsequent session. Guide them with questions such as Do you know what your name means? How was your name chosen? How important is your name to you? When you use your name, how do you use it? Do you like other people to use your full name or a shortened version or do you have a favourite nickname?

In the circle start by telling name stories in pairs. Each pair then takes turns to introduce their partner to the group and say one thing they remembered about that child's name story.

Adaptations Research middle names.

In smaller groups take time to hear each child's name story in the circle.

Reflection Do you know anyone else with the same name as you? Are they anything like you or are they very different? How many children have names that are a 'family' name, given to successive generations perhaps? How do they feel about that?

What did children find interesting about each other's name stories?

Notes

Splodge tag

⑤
🕐 10 mins
🚹🚹🚹
🗨

☑ cooperation
☑ coordination
☑ self-control

How to play — The game starts in the same way as a normal tag game. The first player to be the 'tagger' runs after the rest of the group. When he or she manages to tag another player they join hands. These two players then try to tag a third and then a fourth player who also join up with them. As soon as there is a group of four players together, they split into two sets and each set goes off to tag two more players and so on until there is only one person left who has not yet been tagged. If the game is to continue this player starts off as the new tagger.

Adaptation ⑧ — The 'splodge' does not split but just keeps growing bigger and bigger until all the children are part of one big splodge.

Reflection — This game only works well if players cooperate fully with each other. Was it difficult or easy for small groups to cooperate? How did you decide in which direction to run? Were you all trying to run at the same pace? What were the small splodges trying to do? Was it important to stay together or to catch someone else?

Notes

Group drawing

⑦
🕐 15 mins
🚶 🚶 🚶
💬

☑ cooperation
☑ concentration
☑ sharing
☑ imagination

☑ observation

How to play   Set out large sheets of paper on tables so that groups of children can move around their table easily. Each group draws a collaborative picture or just makes 'marks' on the paper, using a variety of pencils, pastels and pens. The group coordinator can provide a theme or leave the children to draw whatever they like.

Adaptation   Draw pictures in pairs. Divide a piece of paper in two so that pairs can draw at the same time or take turns.

Reflection   How do we maintain group cooperation?

What does it feel like to draw a joint picture? How did you feel when someone drew their image very close to yours or changed your image in some way? What was the difference between all drawing different things on the same piece of paper and all drawing a truly collaborative picture?

Notes

Musical balance

⑦
🕐 5 mins
 † † †
♀

☑ cooperation
☑ trust
☑ self-awareness

This game needs at least twelve people in the circle for it to work successfully.

How to play
Players form a circle with each person holding on to the waist of the person in front of them. They walk around while music is playing. When the music stops they have to sit down gently on the lap of the person behind them. The circle usually collapses the first few times but most groups can eventually manage this very successfully.

Adaptations
Play musical chairs but instead of players being 'out' when chairs are removed, they can balance on another person's lap so there will be more and more people sitting on each chair and they will have to balance carefully.

In pairs, players sit back to back on the floor with their knees bent. They then link arms and try to stand up together.

Reflection
It's OK to make mistakes or for things to not quite work out. By persevering and altering the way we approach the task or by improving our skills we can often solve the problem. Does this game involve a problem or a challenge?

Notes

Vocal orchestra

⑥
🕐 10 mins
🚶 🚶 🚶
💬

☑ cooperation
☑ negotiation
☑ non-verbal
communication

☑ concentration
☑ observation

How to play   The game coordinator demonstrates how to 'conduct' an orchestra with hand movements that indicate, e.g. loudly/softly, quickly/slowly, all join in, stop.

Each child chooses a vocalization (see *Guess the voice*, page 60). Players stand in a row, in small groups or in a circle according to the size of the group. Conductors take turns to conduct the orchestra as a whole group and with duos, solos etc.

Adaptations   Use movements instead of sounds, e.g. hop, jump, stretch, wave.

⑤

Divide the group up into smaller groups of four before starting. The smaller groups stand together and all do the action or make the same sound when the conductor points to them.

Use home-made instruments.

Reflection   What does it feel like to be the conductor? What does it feel like to be part of the orchestra? What are some of the difficulties involved in being a conductor? What does it feel like to do a solo or duo when you are part of an orchestra?

Do all cooperative games need a leader?

Notes

Talking heads

⑨
🕐 10 mins

☑ cooperation   ☑ anticipation
☑ negotiation
☑ taking turns
☑ concentration

How to play   In pairs, children put one arm round each other and act as if they were one person. They talk about a given subject, with each person saying one word at a time to make sentences. This means that they have to guess what the other person is aiming to say and it can get quite frustrating and difficult! Topics could include 'Why I like chocolate', 'What I did yesterday', 'My favourite holiday', 'What I learned at school this morning'.

Adaptation   The audience asks questions and the pair have to answer one word at a time.

Reflection   Did pairs manage to cooperate to make sense even if they couldn't guess what their partner was going to say? Sometimes we think we know what other people are thinking. Sometimes we expect others to know what we are thinking!

Notes

Big ball parachute game

⑤
10 mins

☑ cooperation
☑ concentration
☑ observation

How to play Players hold the parachute at waist level and send a very large ball around the circle. One half of the players aim to try and keep the ball in the circle while the other half try and send it out.

Adaptation Send several different sized balls around the circle, either with everyone cooperating to try to keep the balls going in the same direction or with half the group trying to send the balls out of the circle.

Reflection Talk about cooperating as a large group. What are some of the real life situations where groups of children might need to cooperate? What happens when some members of the group are not cooperating?

Notes

Working parts

⑥
15 mins
🚹🚹🚹
🗨🗨

☑ cooperation
☑ negotiation
☑ problem-solving
☑ creative thinking
☑ observation

You may need to brainstorm some ideas for machines with the group before you start the game (e.g. a CD in a CD player, lawnmower, motorbike, computer with mouse, mobile phone).

How to play: Small teams (around five is a good number) think of a machine that has several working parts. Each member of the team takes on the role of a different part in the machine (and an 'operator'). Players can use sounds and actions and have parts working together or at different times.

Each team practises their machine and then demonstrates it for the other teams to guess what it is.

Adaptations: Teams pick a machine from a prepared set of cards.

Teams invent a machine and explain it to the rest of the group.

Reflection: Did all team members take an equal part? Is it possible for teams to be non-competitive? Did teams have a leader or did all members join in with the decision-making?

Notes

Abandon ship!

⑨
🕐 **30 mins**
♀ ♀ ♀
♡♡♡

☑ negotiation   ☑ problem-solving
☑ compromise
☑ cooperation
☑ creative thinking

How to play	Split into an equal number of small groups or pairs, according to the size of the whole group. Within each group members imagine that they are on a ship that is about to sink. They have a lifeboat but they are only allowed to take ten items with them from the ship. First they think of ten items each. They then have to negotiate with other team members as to what to take as they can only take ten items between them. Groups then join with another group and renegotiate the ten items. Eventually the whole group meet and negotiate a final ten items.
Adaptation	The whole group has been shipwrecked. They have two empty plastic bottles to use on the desert island. Small groups or pairs think of as many uses as possible for the two bottles. The whole group then pool their ideas.
Reflection	How did it feel? Is everyone happy with the final decision? Is everyone happy with how the negotiations went? Did everyone get a chance to put their ideas forward? In the final group did a clear leader emerge? How easy or difficult was it to agree on ten items? What are some of the benefits of working in a group to solve problems?
Notes	

Skill swap

⑩
🕐 30 mins
🧍 🧍
💬💬

☑ cooperation   ☑ sharing
☑ negotiation
☑ problem-solving
☑ asking questions

How to play   The group is divided into two teams. Each team is given a large sheet of paper on which to make a collage or painting to represent a theme such as 'dance' or 'music'. Team A is given all the materials needed for the activity (coloured paper, paint etc.) but no equipment. Team B is given all the equipment (paint brushes, scissors, glue, sticky tape etc.) but no collage materials. The two teams need to negotiate with each other in order to make their collages.

Adaptation   The theme for the collages could represent a conflict situation such as dealing with bullying.

Reflection   What happened during the trading? What worked? What didn't work?

Notes

Additional notes: more ideas for cooperation and negotiation

Reflections

13

In the driving seat: being in control, managing stress and tolerating frustration

Sleeping bear

⑤
🕐 10 mins
🧍 🧍 🧍
💬

☑ self-awareness
☑ self-control
☑ listening
☑ waiting

☑ tolerating
   frustration

A game to heighten concentration and self-awareness.

How to play   The game coordinator chooses the first person to be the bear. This person sits on a chair in the middle of the circle or at the far end of the room, blind-folded. A bunch of keys is placed under the chair. The game coordinator chooses a player to creep up to the chair and steal the keys before the bear can point at him or her. If they manage to get the keys then he or she becomes the new bear.

Adaptation   Two children at a time cross the room from opposite ends. They both keep their eyes shut. One is the hunter and one is the bear. They must both move slowly and cautiously and listen out for each other.

Reflection   Talk about self-control and self-awareness. Talk about the difference between listening with full attention and hearing noises without fully attending.

Notes

All birds fly

⑥
🕐 5 mins
† † †
♀

☑ self-awareness
☑ self-control
☑ tolerating
   frustration

☑ concentration
☑ observation

How to play   This is another version of 'Simon says'. The aim is for the caller to 'catch players out' by getting them to flap their arms at the wrong time. A chosen player starts the game by flapping his or her arms like a bird and saying 'all birds fly'. All other players in the group flap their arms in response. The caller then names a mixture of birds, animals and objects in random order, flapping his or her arms every time e.g. 'eagles fly', 'sparrows fly', 'monkeys fly', 'chairs fly', 'crows fly'. The rest of the group should only flap their arms when a bird is called. If any player flaps when an animal or an object is called they have to stand still for the next two calls.

Each caller has ten turns before handing over to another caller.

Adaptations   The same game could be played with 'all fish swim'. The caller makes a swimming gesture with one arm.

The time for 'standing still' can be extended so that children experience waiting for longer periods.

Reflection   Was this easy or difficult? What helped you to control your responses? What were you feeling when you were waiting to join in again?

Notes

Sleeping monsters

⑤
🕐 10 mins
† † †
♡

☑ self-awareness
☑ self-control
☑ waiting

This is a very slight adaptation of the familiar game of 'sleeping lions'.

How to play The monsters are stamping around the room with heavy footsteps until they are suddenly very tired and have to lie down on the ground and close their eyes. The game coordinator walks quietly around the room to see if they are all really asleep. The coordinator can talk but must not touch the monsters. If any monsters are seen to move then they must get up and help to spot any others who are moving.

Adaptation Use two different types of music – one very loud with a heavy beat and one quiet and gentle. The monsters move to the sound of the first and lie down when they hear the second.

Reflection Does your breathing change when you are being calm? How does it change? When might it be useful to make your breathing calm on purpose?

Notes

Run like the wind

⑤
🕐 5 mins
🚶 🚶 🚶
💬

☑ self-awareness
☑ self-control
☑ listening
☑ observation

☑ imagination

How to play   Explain to the children that you are the head of a village in the jungle and you are in charge of looking after all the village children while they play. They are an extremely noisy group of children and run like the wind through the jungle, shouting and laughing. The only danger in the jungle is lions! You can hear the lions coming long before the children can. They have to watch you carefully and when you sit down with your hand over your mouth they have to sit down immediately too. Their silence and stillness will trick the lions who will go away. You signal that the danger is passed by shouting 'run like the wind!' Then everyone gets up and runs and shouts again.

Adaptation   Choose new village leaders in a way that no one else knows who has been chosen.

Reflection   How easy or difficult is it to stay aware of what is going on when you are doing something very active?

Notes

This and that

⑤
🕐 5 mins
† † †
💬

☑ self-awareness
☑ self-control
☑ listening
☑ concentration

☑ tolerating
frustration

Another variation of 'Simon says'.

How to play　The game coordinator demonstrates simple movements for players to follow such as stand on one leg, touch your ear, wave, clap. When the instruction is 'do this' then players copy the movement. When the instruction is 'do that' no one is supposed to move. If a player makes a mistake they must stand still for the next two calls.

Adaptations　Instead of standing still when mistakes are made, players continue to join in but move to an inner circle. It is likely that all players will be in this circle before very long!

Play 'Simon says' while holding on to a parachute. Movements will be based on leg, head or whole body movements e.g. stand on one leg, nod your head, shake your shoulders, shake your foot.

Reflection　Talk about self-awareness and self-control. When we repeat something often enough we begin not to notice what we are doing. Why is this useful? When might it not be useful?

Notes

Our story

⑤
🕐 5 mins
👤 👤
💬

☑ self-awareness   ☑ waiting
☑ self-control
☑ listening
☑ concentration

This is a variation of a popular game called 'the old family coach'.

How to play   The game coordinator makes up a short story about the group, using each child's name at least three times. When the child hears their own name they stand up, turn round three times and take a bow! When they hear '*all the children*' or '*everyone*' they all stand up, turn round three times and take a bow.

For example: 'The new classroom was ready at last and *all the children* waited excitedly in the playground on the first day of term. The head teacher asked *Edward* and *Jodie* to fetch the registers from the office. On the way inside they bumped into *Karen* and *Amarjeet* who had gone to fetch the school bell. *Sam* was allowed to ring the bell and he rang it so loudly that *Marcus* and *Sandeep* put their hands over their ears. Then *Edward* and *Michèle* led *everyone* into their new classroom…' and so on.

Adaptations   Use a response that requires only slight or no physical movement.

Use musical instruments for children to signal when they hear their name.

Tell a story about going to the zoo. The children choose an animal and make the appropriate animal noise when they hear their name.

⑦   Base the story around an imaginary incident which caused frustration or anger in someone else (a fictitious teacher for example) and the children have to help out. This version of the activity is particularly effective if the story makes the children laugh. A sense of humour is great for defusing anger if it is timely and appropriate (see also *Consequences* page 85).

Reflection   Saying someone's name is a good way to get their attention. What else is it OK to do when we want to say something to someone who doesn't seem to be listening? What is it *not* OK to do?

What do you feel if you don't hear something important?

Notes

Puppets

⑤   ☑ self-awareness
🕐 5 mins   ☑ self-control
👤 👤 👤   ☑ empathy
💭   ☑ concentration

How to play   Tell the children that they are going to pretend to be puppets. They start in a standing position with their feet firmly on the ground, their arms stretched upwards and fingers spread out as though they are being held up by strings. They imagine that the strings are very slowly being loosened so that their body starts to drop down. Start with just the fingers, then hands, arms, head and upper body, finally bending slightly at the knees. The same movements are then performed in reverse until the children are standing upright again with arms stretched as high as they can. Do this several times at varying speeds.

Adaptation   In pairs take turns at being puppet and puppeteer. Without touching the
⑦   puppet the puppeteer pretends to pull strings to get different parts of the puppet to move in different directions and at different speeds. This works well if the puppet is lying down to start with and the puppeteer has to work out which strings to pull in order to get the puppet to stand up.

Reflection   How does your body move? What aspects of movements can you control (speed, direction, range). Think about the complicated sequence of movements needed to stand up or sit down. How do we learn how to do this? Talk about how children make mistakes and fall over when they are learning but as we get older we move without thinking about it. Can you tell when your muscles are relaxed and when they are tense? Do you ever think about your shoulders, your back, the backs of your knees?

Notes

Musical drawings

⑦   ☑ self-awareness   ☑ self-confidence
🕑 20 mins   ☑ managing stress
♦ ♦ ♦   ☑ listening
🗨   ☑ imagination

How to play   The game coordinator plays a variety of music and the group draws whatever comes to mind while listening to the different rhythms and moods.

Adaptation   Children bring in their own selections of music and talk about how they feel when they listen to it.

Reflection   Talk about how music can affect our mood. Is there a piece of music that always makes you feel sad or always makes you feel happy?

Notes

Pass a smile

⑤
🕐 5 mins
♟ ♟
💬

- ☑ self-awareness
- ☑ managing stress
- ☑ non-verbal communication

- ☑ taking turns
- ☑ concentration

How to play   Players sit in a circle. Everyone tries to look very solemn. A child is chosen to start off a smile. He sends a smile to the person sitting next to him. This person smiles then 'zips' their lips in order to 'hold' the smile. He then turns to the next person and unzips the smile to pass it on! When the smile has been around the circle once, the group have a go at passing another smile but this time even more quickly.

Adaptation   'Throw' a smile across the circle. Everyone has to stay on the alert to catch it!

Reflection   Talk about how it is possible to sometimes have control over how we feel. How does your body feel when you smile? What makes you smile? Can you tell the difference between a genuine smile and a pretend one or an 'unkind' smile? *How* can you tell the difference?

Notes

Melting snowman

⑤
🕐 5 mins
† † †
💬

☑ self-awareness
☑ self-control
☑ relaxation skills
☑ imagination

☑ dramatic
   awareness

How to play
Spread out around the room so that each child has plenty of space in which to 'melt'. Players start by imagining that they are a newly built snowman. They stand very still with their arms by their sides. Each child makes all their muscles tense. Now they imagine the sun has come out and it is getting warmer and warmer. The snowmen start to 'melt' until they are pools of melted snow on the floor. The children lie very still, letting all their muscles go floppy. Now the snow clouds come and lots of snow falls so that they can be built up into snowmen again. Melt once more. Then they are back to being children again. Ask them to stand up tall and shake their arms, hands and legs as if they are shaking the snow off.

Adaptation
Alternate between being a rag doll and a wooden or metal toy.

Reflection
What does it feel like to be tense and what does it feel like to be very relaxed? Notice the difference between being very tense as a snowman and feeling strong without feeling excessive tension. Why is it important for our bodies to be relaxed sometimes? Is there such a thing as useful tension? When do we need to be tense? Are there times when you have tension in your body that doesn't need to be there?

Notes

Worry stories

⑧
🕐 50 mins
🧍 🧍 🧍
💬 💬 💬

☑ managing stress
☑ listening
☑ cooperation

☑ sequencing/
   story-telling
☑ planning

How to play   Make a group list of things that children might worry about at school or when playing with friends. Small groups of children are invited to make up a short story about 'the day the worries took over our school'. They practise this together, taking an equal share in the telling. The groups then take turns to tell their story to the whole group.

Adaptation   Groups make up a short play involving a detective who has been sent to a small town where worries have taken over all the adults. The detective interviews a teacher, a doctor, a baker, a fireman, a factory worker, a builder etc. Each person is *very* worried about everything to do with their job!

Reflection   Do you think everyone has worries? Do people worry about the same sorts of things? Are some worries useful? What happens when worries take up a lot of thinking time and aren't resolved? Who do you share worries with? What could you do with your worries?

Notes

Giggle switch

⑤
⏱ 5 mins
♀ ♀ ♀
💬

☑ managing stress
☑ self-awareness
☑ self-control
☑ taking turns

☑ eye contact

How to play   Pairs sit facing each other. They choose who is A and who is B. They must keep eye contact and try to keep a straight face. The game coordinator waits until everyone is quiet and then says 'giggle switch', at which point person A tries to make person B giggle in any way they can without touching them. At any time the coordinator can say 'giggle switch' again and the players have to swap roles.

Adaptations   The children lie down on the floor in a circle with heads nearly touching in the centre and feet facing towards the outside of the circle, their hands resting gently on their stomachs. The first person starts off by saying 'ha!', the second says 'ha ha!', the third says 'ha ha ha!', and so on, going as fast as possible until someone starts to laugh for real. Then everyone has to wait for silence before another child starts off a round of 'ho!' This can also be played with each child lying with their head on someone else's stomach. The movement involved in saying 'ha!' can cause laughter before the round gets very far at all!

Reflection   Talk about the importance of laughter. How do you feel when you have had a 'fit of the giggles'? Talk about the difference between 'laughing at someone' and 'laughing with someone'. Laughter can have very different qualities and can therefore cause us to feel quite differently too.

Notes

Shake it out

⑦
🕐 10 mins
�;
♀♀

☑ managing stress   ☑ trust
☑ self-awareness
☑ creative thinking
☑ taking turns

How to play   Make a list of 'difficult' feelings (e.g. anger, sadness, jealousy, frustration, being fed up). Brainstorm ideas for what to do with these feelings (e.g. when I feel angry I can tell someone, do something active to get rid of the tension in my body, scribble in a scribble book etc.)

Do rounds of 'I feel angry when…', etc. After each round, end with a shake to release any tension. Everyone shakes their arms and legs and shoulders. Finish with a round of 'When difficult feelings come I know how to…'

Adaptation   Each child pretends their fingers are having a mock fight, scrabbling around
⑤   each other moving very fast, clasping hands together, feeling the tightness. Now change to 'floating' fingers, gently and slowly moving around each other, one hand stroking the other. Change back and forth two or three times and then eventually hands float down to rest in the child's lap.

Reflection   Difficult feelings come and go. Feelings don't last for ever. Just because we might feel angry now doesn't mean that we are always going to be an angry person. These feelings are normal. It is good to know how to handle them.

Notes

Additional notes: more ideas for self-control, stress management and tolerating frustrations

Reflections

14

Got it! Problem-solving

Sort us out

⑦
🕐 10 mins
👤👤👤
💬💬

☑ problem-solving
☑ cooperation
☑ memory
☑ categorization

☑ asking questions
☑ observation

How to play The game coordinator times the group while they arrange themselves in a line according to one or more of the following criteria:

- alphabetically according to the first letter of their first name

- according to house number

- according to age

- according to what time they get up in the morning.

Adaptations The children choose their own criteria for organizing the group into a line.

Smaller groups of children stand on a PE bench and then try to arrange themselves according to different criteria without stepping off the bench.

The game is played with criteria chosen that do not need any verbal interaction (e.g. height, groups of children with same eye colour or hair colour).

Reflection Which line took the least time to organize? Why? Which grouping took the longest? Why?

Think about similarities and differences and how we could be members of several different groups. How does it feel to be a member of a particular group of friends? What is it like to be part of more than one group? What are some of the good things about being in different groups? When is it not so helpful to have separate groupings or gangs?

Notes

Tangled up

⑤
🕐 10 mins
👤 👤 👤
💬

☑ problem-solving   ☑ observation
☑ cooperation
☑ creative thinking
☑ self-awareness

A well-known problem-solving game which children never seem to get tired of playing!

How to play   The whole group joins hands to form a chain. The person at one end begins to weave in and out, leading other members into a 'tangle' without breaking the links. Players can go over/under arms; between legs etc. Two players then try to untangle the group by giving instructions only. They cannot touch the chain at all.

Adaptation   Children stand in a circle then close their eyes and stretch out their hands to find other hands. They then open their eyes and try to untangle themselves without letting go.

Reflection   How did it feel to be in the role of problem-solver?

What were the important things to remember so that the chain did not break and no one got hurt? Have you ever come across problems that seemed too complex to unravel at first? How should we tackle that sort of problem?

Notes

Cooperative story-telling

⑧
🕐 10 mins

☑ problem-solving
☑ cooperation
☑ listening
☑ sequencing

☑ creative thinking
☑ waiting

How to play
The first player starts off a story by stating a 'problem' that needs to be solved. The next player continues the story by saying one or two sentences. The third player adds one or two more sentences and so on around the circle. The aim is for the last person in the circle to bring the story to a satisfactory conclusion while still only using two sentences at the most. A new problem is then introduced.

The game continues for as long as all players remain engaged.

Adaptation
The group is given a selection of catchphrases or objects which must be incorporated into the story in a cohesive way. Players may choose these at random or they have to follow a pattern such as 'every third person in the circle picks an object to include in their part of the story'. The game coordinator can challenge unconvincing connections.

Reflection
Was this easy or difficult? Were players helping each other out? If so, how did they do that?

Were there creative solutions to problems?

Does it help to have more than one person solving a problem? Did other players have different solutions that they didn't get the chance to share?

Notes

Step up

⑤
🕐 15 mins
👤 👤 👤
💬💬

☑ problem-solving   ☑ creative thinking
☑ cooperation
☑ listening
☑ trust

This game requires a large space and a supply of 'stepping stones'
made from paper or card.

How to play   Small groups of around six to eight players per group must cross the desig-
nated space by using a small number of stepping stones (not enough to get
them all the way across the space). No member of the group is allowed to
touch the ground or floor. Five or six stones are normally enough for a group
of eight.

Adaptation   Groups use the stepping stones to 'rescue' a player who is stranded on the
⑧   other side of the space. The stranded player is blindfolded. If he or she comes
off a stepping stone and touches any part of the floor the rescue has to start
from the beginning again.

Reflection   Was there more than one way to solve the problem? How did group members
cooperate? How did it feel to be the stranded player? Did you feel safe? What
helped you to trust the group?

Notes

Transportation

⑧   ☑ problem-solving   ☑ creative thinking
⏱ 10 mins   ☑ cooperation
👤👤👤   ☑ tolerating
💬💬   frustration

How to play   Small groups of players (four to six per group) are given a set of small objects
              of various shapes and weights which they must transport from one side of the
              room to the other. Each player can only use one finger of one hand and must
              keep the other hand behind their back. The aim is to move the objects within
              a set time limit (decided according to the dexterity of the players and the
              number of objects being used).

Adaptation   If an object is dropped the players must start from the beginning again.

Reflection   What do you feel when you solve a problem either individually or as a group?
              What skills are involved in problem-solving? Do you feel comfortable asking
              for help when something is difficult?

Notes

Find the leader

⑤
🕐 10 mins
👤 👤 👤
💬

☑ problem-solving   ☑ observation
☑ non-verbal
   communication
☑ concentration

How to play   One person (the detective) leaves the room while the others choose a leader. The detective returns and stands in the middle of the circle. Players in the circle have to copy everything the leader does and the detective tries to spot who the leader is.

Adaptation   Have two leaders and two detectives. The leaders lead alternate players in the circle.

Reflection   How do leaders ensure they have the attention of the players? Does everyone watch the leader or is it sometimes a chain reaction? Talk about leading by example and leading by instruction.

Notes

Additional notes: more ideas for problem-solving

Reflections

Off we go! Setting goals and being prepared

Bravery awards

⑤
🕐 15 mins
♦ ♦ ♦
💬💬

☑ self-awareness
☑ trust
☑ taking turns
☑ respecting others

☑ giving and
   receiving praise

How to play   Talk about times when we do something a *little* bit scary that might take some courage. Suggest very 'ordinary' situations (e.g. first day at a new school, learning to ride a bike, diving into the pool for the first time, reading aloud in the school play). Encourage children to think up at least ten situations. Think about what sorts of things made these situations easier to handle. Now brainstorm ways in which we acknowledge someone else's bravery. This could be verbal praise, thumbs up, clapping etc. or a full award ceremony. Do a round of 'I was brave when…' with each child choosing one situation from the list. The rest of the group acknowledge the child's bravery noisily and enthusiastically!

Adaptation   Acknowledge small triumphs of mastery; times of making a 'wise decision'; times of solving a problem.

Reflection   Talk about learning to notice our own small achievements and praising ourselves. Sometimes other people don't notice or don't know how we feel or what we've achieved. Just because they don't praise us doesn't mean that we didn't do well.

What skills do you have that will help you to be prepared for future challenges?

Notes

I packed my suitcase

⑧
🕐 10 mins
👤 👤 👤
💬💬

☑ being prepared
☑ listening
☑ memory
☑ taking turns

☑ creative thinking

This is a familiar memory game adapted to help children to think carefully about what they might need for different situations.

How to play   Brainstorm a variety of different activities or adventures that would need different equipment and clothing as well as items that would be relevant for any situation (for example, mountaineering, deep sea diving, going to an adventure playground, visiting a hot country, visiting a cold country, going on a treasure hunt).

Choose one of these and play a round of 'I packed my suitcase and I took…' Each child has to remember what has already been packed and add one more item to the list. When the list gets too long to remember, choose another adventure and start again.

Adaptation   Older children can challenge the inclusion of an item that doesn't seem relevant for the particular adventure.

Reflection   How can we prepare ourselves for adventures and challenges? If we think something is going to be scary, embarrassing or difficult what could we do to help ourselves to cope with this?

Notes

Adverts

ⅹ
🕐 50 mins
† † †
ᗉᗉᗉ

☑ setting goals
☑ creative thinking
☑ cooperation

☑ understanding
   characteristics
☑ self-awareness

This game helps children to recognize and explore some of the skills and attributes that they have in relation to different aspects of their lives.

How to play Each player chooses a 'role' from a provided list. This could be a role that they actually play in life or one they would like to play. This works best if at least three children choose each role. Players are then grouped together according to their choices and cooperate to design a joint poster or TV advert for themselves in this particular role, highlighting skills and attributes. Volunteers share their posters in the circle.

Possible roles might be: sports ace, computer expert, brother/sister, son/daughter, friend, artist, science whiz kid, inventor, builder.

Adaptation Design 'your class needs you' posters highlighting attributes and skills needed for successful group work.

Reflection Everyone has valuable skills and attributes. What skill or attribute are you most proud of? What is the difference between boasting and being proud about something? (Boasting and 'putting others down' can be how some children express anger when their own feelings of self-worth are low.)

Notes

Emblems of success

⑦
🕐 45 mins
👤 👤 👤
💬

☑ understanding metaphors
☑ being prepared
☑ deduction

☑ self-awareness
☑ self-respect

How to play   Players each draw the shape of a shield on a large piece of paper. They divide the shield into four sections and draw different symbols or pictures in each section to show successful strategies that they have used for anger management. Some possible strategies are:

- talking with a friend
- asking for help to solve the difficulty
- listening to some relaxing music
- respecting and valuing myself
- respecting and valuing other people
- walking away from conflict situations
- finding a quiet space to 'chill out'.

Display the shields on a table or wall. Players guess the owner of each one.

Adaptations   Draw a shield for my hopes for next year or my motto.

Make one large coat of arms for the whole group.

Make a flag instead of a shield.

Reflection   Talk about similarities and differences between the shields.

Talk about and celebrate times when children have used strategies successfully.

Notes

Variety show

ⓘ
🕐 30 mins
♦ ♦ ♦
💬

☑ setting goals
☑ self-awareness
☑ trust
☑ creative thinking

☑ self-respect

Players will need to have plenty of preparation time before this game.

How to play   Invite the children (volunteers) to take turns in showing the rest of the group something that creatively expresses how they manage strong emotions. This can be an object chosen from home (such as a photograph, a book, a favourite toy); a short piece of music (drum beats, a well known song); a drawing; a dance; a single movement; a short story; a poem – absolutely anything at all! There is no interpretation needed unless the children want to explain the relevance of what they have chosen. The children each give their presentation and the group respond with applause and praise.

Adaptation   Players choose something they are wearing or something they have with them on the day (i.e. no preparation) and say in what way it reflects their own personality and then how this aspect of their personality is going to help them in managing angry feelings.

Reflection   Different strategies work for different people.

Sometimes just thinking about a person or an object or a calm place can help us to feel calm or more in control of our feelings.

Notes

Pack your suitcase

⑧
🕐 5 mins
👤 👤 👤
💬💬

☑ imagination
☑ dramatic
    awareness

☑ understanding
    metaphors
☑ empathy

How to play   Players are invited to imagine that they each have a suitcase or treasure box
that they are going to take away with them when they leave the group. They
can choose whatever they want to put into it – perhaps a memory of a particular event or of people in the group, a skill they have developed, a new game
that they have learned or something important that someone said to them.
Ask each child in turn or ask for volunteers to say what they will pack in their
suitcase to take away with them.

Adaptation   Players sit in a circle. Each child takes an imaginary gift from a treasure chest
in the centre of the circle and presents it to the person sitting next to them,
saying what the gift is and why they are giving it to that person.

Reflection   How will you remind yourself of your achievements? Sometimes we carry
heavy suitcases of worries and troubles with us everywhere we go. Try experi-
menting with carrying *this* suitcase for a while instead!

Notes

Additional notes: more ideas for goal-setting

Reflections

16

Wind-downs and celebrations

Parachute wind-downs

If you have been using a parachute for some of the games try the following:

- Invite all the children to lie still under the parachute while game coordinators gently waft it up and down over the top of them.
- Sit around the outside edge of the parachute and pass a smile or a hand squeeze around the circle.
- Invite the children to lie quietly on top of the parachute, listening to some gentle music or a short story.

Relaxation

⑤   ☑ self-calming
⏱ 20 mins   ☑ listening
♦ ♦ ♦   ☑ self-distraction
♡   ☑ body awareness

This type of relaxation works by focusing the mind on different areas of the body and just being aware of what that area feels like. Often if we try to relax, we try too hard! In our efforts to relax we actually set up more tension. By observing what the body is doing there is a natural tendency simply to allow any areas of tension to relax and release.

What to do   The children can be lying down (e.g. on top of a parachute) or seated. Read each part very slowly and calmly with plenty of pauses to allow everyone time to follow your instructions.

Instructions   When you are ready, let your eyes close gently and settle yourself into a comfortable position.

Notice the feel of your body on the floor (in the chair)…now start to notice your feet… Put all your attention on your feet and really notice what they feel like. Maybe they feel warm or cold; perhaps they are numb or itchy…tight or relaxed. Just notice whatever you can feel in your feet…

Now gently move your thoughts from your feet to the lower part of your legs. Let your thoughts leave your feet and just move very easily to your legs. Notice whatever feeling is there just at this moment… There are no right or wrong feelings… Whatever you can feel is OK…

Now move up to your knees…and then the top part of your legs and notice whatever feelings are there… Now start to notice your body, feel what's happening when you breathe gently in and out…start to think about your shoulders…feel any tightness just melt away… Notice all the feelings around your neck and your head…

Let your thoughts go gently to your back…all along the length of your back…feel the relaxation spreading through your body… Thinking about your arms now. Just notice whatever is there…and down the length of your arms into your hands… Notice all your fingers one by one. Whatever is there, just notice it…

Now, instead of thinking of yourself in parts, feel your whole body relax. Just letting go…letting the floor (chair) support you and just relaxing into it… As you breathe in, breathe in relaxation…and feel it spreading through every part of you…breathing in…and out…like waves on a sea shore… Lie quietly for a few moments and enjoy the feeling of being relaxed…

(Allow at least one or two minutes of quietness)

Keep noticing your body and start to listen to whatever sounds there are around you… Begin to move your hands and feet a little bit… When you feel ready, open your eyes and look around you… Lie or sit quietly for a short while before stretching and having a yawn…

Source: *Helping Children to Build Self-esteem*, (2nd edn) (Plummer 2007)

Reflection   Sometimes if we are very anxious or nervous or tense about something it shows in our body. Our muscles become tight. Maybe they begin to ache a little bit. We might feel 'knotted up' inside. This can feel very uncomfortable. It's a really nice feeling to be able to relax your body and it will help you to feel confident and more able to do things that are a bit difficult.

Notes

Pass the shell

⑦
🕐 5 mins
† † †
◯◯

☑ listening
☑ trust
☑ empathy
☑ taking turns

☑ giving and
   receiving praise

How to play   Use a large shell or a beautiful/unusual object of some sort. Pass the shell around the group. Whoever is holding it praises someone else and passes them the shell. This is best done in sequence around the circle to start with until you feel that children can praise each other in random order and not leave anyone out.

Adaptations   Each child has a piece of paper and writes their name at the bottom. The papers are passed around the group for everyone to write something positive about the person named on the paper. The paper is folded over after each comment has been added so that no one sees what anyone else has written. The paper is then returned to the original player to read when they want to.

Everyone has a piece of paper pinned to their back for others to write praises on.

Reflection   What does it feel like to give and receive praise? How many different ways can we praise each other? What would you most like to be praised for? What do you think your mother/brother/best friend would most like to be praised for? Is there anything you *don't* like to be praised for?

Notes

Closing circles

⑦
🕐 **5 mins**
♀ ♀ ♀
💬💬

☑ listening
☑ trust
☑ taking turns
☑ concentration

☑ self-awareness

How to play   At the end of each meeting bring everyone back together again in a circle and finish with each person having the chance to say one brief thing before they leave. For example:

- I feel…

- Today I found out that…

- Today I felt…

- My name is…and I am…

- I have noticed that…

- I feel really good about…

Adaptation   Play a version of *Feel it, do it* (see page 89) where, instead of saying their name with various emotions, the children do a round of 'I'm brilliant at…' or 'I feel really good about…', expressing the appropriate emotion strongly through body language and facial expression for others to reflect back.

Reflection   Do you set yourself goals to work towards? What would you most like to achieve by the end of next week? Next month? Next term? How will you know when you've achieved it? How will other people know that you've achieved it?

Notes

Big group yell

⑤

⏱ 5 mins

👤 👤 👤

💬

☑ listening
☑ cooperation
☑ self-awareness

How to play   Everyone crouches down together in a huddle. The game coordinator begins a low humming sound and the others join in. As the whole group gradually stands up, the noise level gets louder and louder until everyone jumps into the air and yells as loudly as they can.

Adaptations   Everyone crouches down in a circle facing inwards. Everyone hums quietly and then gradually gets louder as they all stand up together and raise their arms above their heads. Then everyone does the reverse – starting with a loud hum and getting quieter and quieter as they sink down to the ground and eventually they lie down with their feet towards the centre of the circle in complete silence.

Use yogurt-pot shakers to make a crescendo of noise by adding on one person at a time, and then stop one person at a time until there is silence.

Each child makes a noise with something that they have with them – bracelets, crayons, coins, keys. Start slowly, build to a crescendo and then stop one at a time.

Reflection   Talk about beginnings and endings. Talk about sharing experiences in groups and how group games can help us to feel energized and full of confidence.

Notes

Winning the Oscars

⑥
10 mins
👤 👤 👤

☑ self-confidence
☑ giving and receiving praise
☑ dramatic awareness
☑ trust
☑ imagination

How to play Cover a wooden spoon or an artist's figure with tin foil. Present this to each child in turn at an imaginary 'award ceremony' for whatever he or she would most like to have an award for. This could be a past achievement, a future goal or something completely fantastical. Really over-play their achievement. The whole group celebrates each award with plenty of clapping and cheering etc.

Adaptation Players take turns to be a 'national treasure'. The rest of the group take turns to walk up to this person and shake hands or give words of praise or thanks.

Reflection Talk about the importance of noticing and celebrating our real achievements and sometimes giving ourselves a verbal or an actual reward for our hard work. Think of small ways that we can reward ourselves and reward others, e.g. make Dad a cup of tea, clean Jim's bike for him, pat someone on the back, invite friends round for a game of football.

Notes

Pirate's treasure parachute game

⑤
🕐 10 mins
† † †
💬

☑ listening
☑ cooperation
☑ empathy
☑ trust

How to play
Everyone puts one possession in a 'treasure' box. Put the box under the parachute. Players hold the parachute at waist level and make 'waves'. Divers take turns to go under the waves to gather one piece of treasure and return it to its owner.

Adaptation
Retrieve treasure according to different qualities or shape e.g. find something wooden, find something made of metal, find something round.

Reflection
Our talents, abilities, personality characteristics and ideas are all examples of our personal 'treasure'. Do you know what is in your treasure box? Make a list of things that you would like other people to know about you.

Notes

Additional notes: more ideas for wind-downs and celebrations

Reflections

Useful resources

Faupel, A., Herrick, E. and Sharp, P. (1998) *Anger Management. A Practical Guide.* Abingdon and New York: David Fulton Publishers.

Geddes, H. (2006) *Attachment in the Classroom. The Links between Children's Early Experience, Emotional Well-being and Performance in School.* London: Worth Publishing.

Johnson, P. and Rae, T. (1999) *Crucial Skills. An Anger Management and Problem Solving Teaching Programme for High School Students.* Bristol: Lucky Duck Publishing.

Stringer, B. and Mall, M. (1999) *A Solution Focused Approach to Anger Management with Children.* Birmingham: The Questions Publishing Company and Birmingham LEA.

Whitehouse, E. and Pudney, W. (1996) *A Volcano in My Tummy. Helping Children to Handle Anger.* Canada: New Society Publishers.

Subject Index

Author Index

Acknowledgements

The idea for this book was conceived by Stephen Jones, commissioning editor at Jessica Kingsley Publishers.

Children from a primary school in Cambridgeshire provided inspiration for the art work. Their insightful depictions of different angry feelings reflect their high degree of emotional awareness. What fabulous kids! My grateful thanks go to them and to their parents for permission to use these illustrations.

A few of the games have been chosen specifically for this collection of anger management games from resource books, and of these I have found books by Mildred Masheder (*Let's Play Together*), Donna Brandes and Howard Phillips (*Gamesters' Handbook*), Arnold Arnold (*The World Book of Games*) and Marian Liebmann (*Art Therapy for Groups*) the most useful. For the majority of the games however I am unable to acknowledge original sources as they have been passed on to me by colleagues or have been adapted from familiar party games. Thanks must therefore go to the many game-players who have been kind enough to share their favourites with me over the years and who so enthusiastically keep the tradition of children's games alive in all its diversity.